DIGITAL
HANDMADE

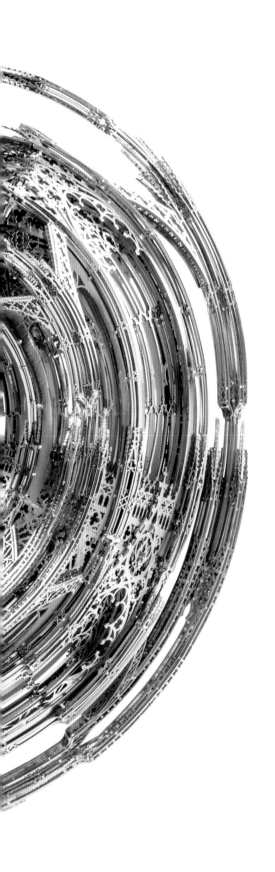

DIGITAL
HANDMADE

CRAFTSMANSHIP AND THE
NEW INDUSTRIAL REVOLUTION

LUCY JOHNSTON

*with 541 illustrations
in colour and black and white*

CONTENTS

INTRODUCTION

'The astounding growth that our resources have undergone in terms of their precision and adaptability will in the near future confront us with very radical changes indeed in the ancient industry of the beautiful . . . Neither matter nor space nor time is what it always was. We must be prepared for such profound changes to alter the entire technological aspect of the arts, influencing invention itself.'

PAUL VALÉRY, *PIÈCES SUR L'ART*, 1931

'By the machine we mean an instrument of mass production. In a sense, every tool is a machine – the hammer, the axe and the chisel. And every machine is a tool . . . The problem is to decide whether the objects of machine production can possess the essential qualities of art.'

HERBERT READ, *ART AND INDUSTRY*, 1934

'It is impossible to accept the view that any essential antagonism exists between art and industry, between beauty and the machine . . . But it is necessary to reintegrate the worlds of art and industry, for only on that basis can we progress towards a new and vital civilization.'

DESIGN RESEARCH UNIT, 1942-72

A RENAISSANCE
IN THE ART OF MAKING

At first glance, the term 'digital handmade' might appear a strange
pairing of words, a contradiction of principles – the ever-rational nature
of computer technologies seemingly mismatched with the passion
and imagination of the craftsman. But as the examples in this book
demonstrate, in the right hands these two contrasting approaches
are combining in new ways to spark a renaissance in the art of
making beautiful, bespoke objects.

Two centuries ago the first industrial revolution revealed a new
order, refining, accelerating and regulating the process of manufacturing
objects for wider appreciation and consumption. This period of
technological innovation resulted in a diminished role for the craftsman
within such a mechanized environment, and ultimately led to the
mass-production construct as we know it today.

But now, as so often seen throughout the history of artistic endeavour,
industrial technologies are informing a new creative movement – the
result of the maturing of a new industrial revolution brought about
by digital technologies. This revolution sees the skill and vision of the
craftsman once again anchored at the heart of a making process, but
using new technologies to free that process from the confines of mass
production and move towards on-demand manufacture and individual
expression on a mass scale.

No longer dictating or restricting the creativity of the making
process, computer software, digital technologies and the tools of large-
scale manufacture are instead being applied in unconventional ways
to enhance and assist it, enabling the crafting of extraordinary, artistic
forms that would previously have been all but impossible.

Combining skilled and often highly time-sensitive manipulation of
these new technologies alongside the tools of tradition, the pioneers of
the movement – the 'digital artisans' – are producing individual, crafted
products of exceptional quality that retain the soul of the material and
the skill of the human hand, while also benefitting from the precision,
efficiency and increasingly unrestricted structural parameters of
digital design and fabrication. This is a landscape where the notion
of machine-assisted making truly becomes an art form.

A STORY OF BEAUTY
AND THE MACHINE

In his utopian novel *News From Nowhere* (1890), William Morris wrote of the 'craving for beauty' awakened in the minds of men no longer tied to the production line. As a collective term, the digital-artisan movement is a contemporary embodiment of that feeling – a new age of creative manufacture that pushes the possibilities of making across new horizons, challenging all the tools of the trade, both digital and analogue, and combining a variety of skills and techniques to introduce us to inspiring and compellingly beautiful objects only ever before conceived in the imagination.

More than that, the term – and the concept of digital handmade – describes a new aesthetic for our times; an exacting beauty, achieved only through the fusion of hand and machine, which presents a uniquely modern understanding and exploration of the relationship between designer and maker. Where machine production on its own provides us reliably with the objects we expect to see, the emerging freedom of the craftsman to challenge the tools of the digital revolution, alongside the traditional tools of manufacture, brings an element of creative magic to the process. Through disassembling, manipulating and reassembling the building blocks of material and form, these artisans reveal a certain beauty that would have been impossible to conceive in the age of analogue alone.

A VERY MODERN TOOLBOX
FOR A VERY MODERN CRAFTSMAN

As with any survey of the diverse world of craftsmanship, the digital-artisan movement has no common style or output, but rather a shared commitment to the mastery of making, and the starting point of a common box of tools and materials. The modern toolbox enables these pioneers to push the realms of possibility further, and to more extraordinary ends, with a structural freedom no longer limited in imagination by the previous practical restrictions of material formation, tooling, or even the effects of gravity during the production process.

Through combining the precision and flexibility of the tools of digital fabrication with the visual quality and tactility brought by the traditional tools of craftsmanship, the modern artisan is empowered to take the best of both worlds and create a new one – and with it, introduce a new kind of maker's mark. The terminology is changing, too, as previously industrial-usage words are becoming accepted – celebrated, even – as part of the descriptive language of the 'digital handmade' movement. The iconic phrase of this era of creative manufacturing is undoubtedly

'3D-printing', a sweeping term used increasingly to represent a wide range of object-shaping processes. But this is only one approach of many digital-fabrication techniques and associated software programs in use by visionary creatives, who are taking the tools of big industry and, with exceptional skill and dedication, re-employing them as the tools of bespoke artisanship.

Now terms such as 'CAD-modelling', 'sintering' and 'CNC-milling' sit comfortably alongside 'carving', 'casting' and 'lathing' as the vernacular of the modern toolkit. Such tools allow the modern craftsman – more than ever before – to merge the worlds of art, design, material science and computer programming to challenge our expectations of structural form and aesthetic narrative.

A CABINET OF CURIOSITIES FOR OUR TIME

This book brings together a collection of the work of eighty pioneering designers, artists and craftsmen – the revolutionaries of their industries, world-renowned, established or emerging – who represent all that is authentic, visionary, ingenious and beautiful of the new digital-artisan movement. Some are highlighted as 'icons' – artisans whose body of work, or a single project, has contributed to defining the field and breaking new ground across the last decade and beyond – while others have emerged and joined the movement more recently, bringing with them increasing levels of experimentation and excellence.

A wealth of objects are presented throughout the book, each conceived and made through a multifaceted process of digital and handcrafted skill – each unique to its maker and across the industry, and each bearing a new kind of maker's mark, born of the complex combination of tools available in this era of creative manufacture. The examples range from the accessible and the affordable to the extraordinary and the unbounded – a contrasting collection of pieces to be made on demand, customized for their owners, snapped up in an instant online or viewed as prized trophies in museums, galleries and private collections. Several iconic artists of the digital-handmade movement are noted for their pioneering contributions, and are marked by the symbol (ICON).

Digital Handmade offers an alternative catalogue of the curious – the rare, the unique and the beautiful, contrasted with those examples of mesmerizing quality and vision that give us a glimpse into the future creative manufacturing possibilities of our world.

'Discovering the digital loom has transformed the horizons of my work. It is almost not like weaving at all – it is more like painting with threads. There is so much potential to be creative with the process itself, not just the initial pattern design.'

JEKATERINA APALE

ILLUSTRATING IN PIXELS, COMMUNICATING IN THREADS

ABOVE
Self Portrait, 2010,
25 × 17 cm (10 × 7 in.)

OPPOSITE
Clockwise from top:
Mandarinfish, 2008;
Child, 2008; *She*, 2008, each
150 × 73 cm (59 × 29 in.)

Drawing on a background in graphic design and illustration, textile artist Jekaterina Apale combines the visual qualities of hand-drawing with the tactile, three-dimensional qualities of weaving in her work. She is a leading figure in the promotion of digital Jacquard weaving as an exciting, flexible medium for graphic artists in Latvia, and creates all of her textile patterns in Adobe Photoshop software, translating each design into a weave file, before allocating colours and types of threads to represent each pixel of the digital pattern.

Apale's MA thesis project, the collage-effect triptych *Mandarinfish* (opposite, top), was the first work to be woven on a TC1 Jacquard loom in her home country. This was followed by the illustrative project *She* (opposite, bottom left), which pushes her explorations of translating illustrative styles into threads. More recent works, including *Self Portrait* (left) and *Creatures*, expand her distinctive weaving technique into the realms of cartoon and graffiti-style graphic arts.

Apale presented another industry innovation, created with friend and student Julija Bondarenko, with her *Panda* cartoon, a short stop-motion film in which the individual frames were digitally illustrated, then woven on the Jacquard loom, before each was photographed and compiled into the final film.

LOCATION RIGA, LATVIA **TECHNIQUES** GRAPHIC-DESIGN SOFTWARE, DIGITAL JACQUARD WEAVING **MATERIALS** MIXED-MATERIAL THREADS

ASSA ASHUACH

DIGITAL ARTISTRY MEETS
PERFECT FABRICATION

ABOVE
Lemon Squeezer,
sintered titanium

OPPOSITE
Clockwise from top left:
Femur Stool, polyamide nylon;
Venturi Stool, maple wood
and dark oak veneer; *Venturi
Floor Lounger*, glass-reinforced
plastic and gloss gel-coating

Industrial designer Assa Ashuach's early experiments with 3D-printing techniques produced designs including the organically shaped *Lemon Squeezer* (left), which was originally offered in selective laser-sintered dyed polyamide nylon, and later as a direct metal-printed limited edition in sintered titanium. It was the first of his products that could be reconfigured and sent to production directly by the customer.

Experiments in recreating biological forms through computer simulation resulted in *Femur Stool* (opposite, top left), printed in selective laser-sintered polyamide nylon and developed using an algorithm to remove any redundant material according to stress zones on the surface. The final piece is optimized to carry a load of 120 kg (265 lbs); if the load is changed in the CAD model before fabrication, the shape will change.

The *Venturi* chair collection, inspired by the Venturi fluid-flow effect, further challenged the capabilities of digital fabrication by giving furniture a quality of finish more often seen in advanced automotive manufacture. The red stool and lounger (opposite, bottom) were produced from CAD models in glass-reinforced plastic using a five-axis CNC-milled mould, then airbrushed with a gloss gel-coating and polished to a mirror shine. The wood version of the stool (opposite, right) was CNC-milled in maple, with details picked out in dark oak veneer.

LOCATION LONDON, UK **TECHNIQUES** CAD-MODELLING,
SELECTIVE LASER-SINTERING, CNC-MILLING, HAND-FINISHING
MATERIALS POLYAMIDE NYLON, TITANIUM, GLASS-REINFORCED
PLASTIC, MAPLE AND OAK **WEBSITE** ASSAASHUACH.COM

'Mathematics has become a means to help us create magical tools that cannot exist in a real workshop. I see digital tools being to the designer what the chisel is to the carpenter, but allowing for the wonderful flexibility of experimentation before the material takes shape.'

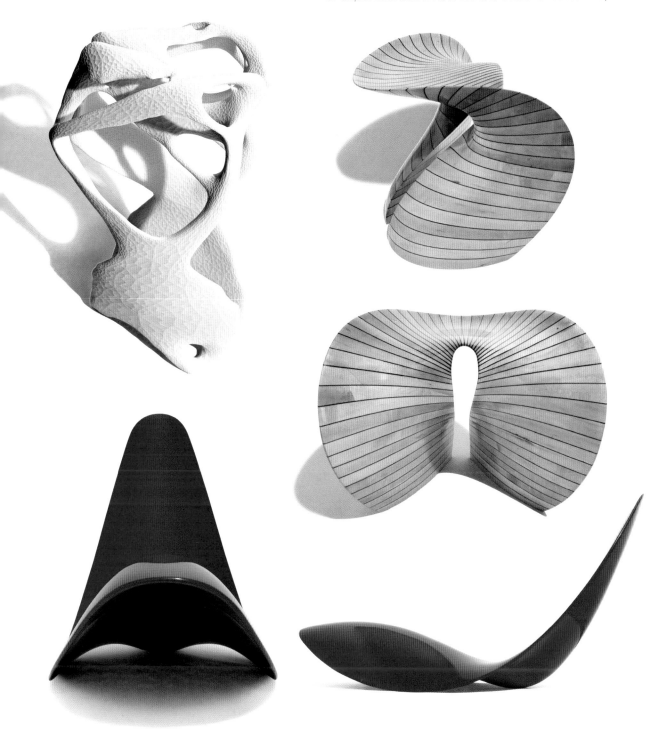

Worldscape is a staggering piece of woodcraft, conceived and executed by architectural studio Atmos, headed by Alex Haw and recognized for its skilled use of new fabrication technologies to craft beautiful, ergonomic environments. The table can seat eighty guests around a three-dimensional map of the planet; diners sit on the ocean shelf and eat off the coastline, lit by cities and in the shadow of mountain ranges.

The geometry of the construction uses the familiar equidistant cylindrical projection of the globe, where all degrees are equal lengths in both directions and plotted with square pixels, a technique known as *plate carrée*. The layered topography of the table was created by plotting the earth's contours onto robust, melamine-faced plywood sheets, which were then cut and precisely inscribed using CNC-routing technology.

The complete table, measuring 14.5 × 7.3 m (48 × 24 ft), consists of thirty-five square modules of irregular landmass, on top of which are the prominent mountainous features of the earth's surface, each formed of vertical cross-sections slotted together with horizontal contours. Cities are represented in the machined detailing by a multitude of pockmarks across the surfaces; the diameter of each drilled hole is determined by a city's degree of light pollution, drawn from NASA satellite images of the world at night. *Worldscape* formed the centrepiece of Global Feast, held during the London 2012 Olympics, and won the Judge's Special Award at the UK Wood Awards 2013.

ATMOS

MAPPING THE WORLD IN SHEETS OF WOOD

LOCATION LONDON, UK **TECHNIQUES** CAD-MODELLING,
CNC-ROUTING **MATERIALS** 12-MM (½-IN.) MELAMINE-COATED
PLYWOOD **WEBSITE** ATMOSSTUDIO.COM

Northern Europe, eaten away by
routed holes of cities (left); the view
down into the Mariana Trench (right)

Looking southwest across China,
with Japan's pockmarked coastline
of cities visible to the left

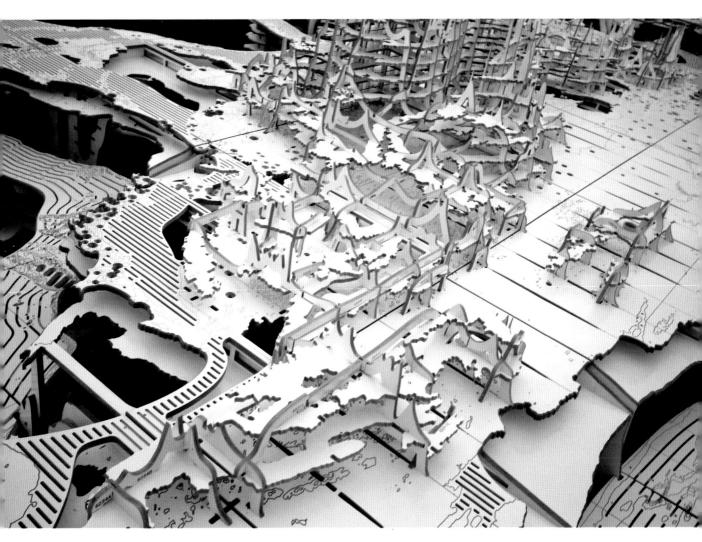

'Digital fabrication is inseparable from craft; you still have to understand the life of the material, empathize with it, anticipate its mood and flux. All tools extend the human body, but also distance it. Digital craftsmanship has brought us back the control of being makers responsible for every detail.'

JORGE AYALA

EXPLORATIONS IN DIGITAL LOGIC AND BIOLOGICAL FORM

THESE PAGES
Cabinet of Post-digital Curiosities, 2013, created through [Ay]A Studio and exhibited at the FRAC Centre, in Orléans, France

Designer Jorge Ayala presents the notion of the post-digital, which appears throughout his work across the fields of art, architecture and fashion design, as a way of combining, rather than separating, digital logic and the biology of natural form.

His career-defining installation, *Cabinet of Post-digital Curiosities* (these pages), was an early exploration into fusing technology, biology, rapid-prototyping and material science, and acted as a platform for experimenting with the generation of new textures and skins. The collection of rapid-prototyped moulds and latex-cast resin organisms was arranged in a grid similar to the periodic table of elements, each with unique skin qualities achieved through varying the parameters applied during the fabrication process, including materials, degradations and chemical reactions.

Ayala launched his fashion label, Jorge Ayala Paris, as an alternative artistic exploration into the development of skins, based around the concept of human ornament and the ability of digital technologies to capture and represent the corresponding ornaments of the natural world in graphic form. His inspiration came from the extravagance of sixteenth-century *nature morte* and the exhibitionist details of the plant and animal kingdoms. The vibrant patterns of his fashion textiles originate from still-life photography, which are deconstructed and evolved to create experimental digital compositions. These are digitally printed at high resolution onto silk fabrics for scarves, dresses, shirts and jackets.

LOCATION PARIS, FRANCE **TECHNIQUES** CAD-MODELLING, RAPID-PROTOTYPING, HAND-MOULDING, DIGITAL PHOTOGRAPHY, GRAPHIC EFFECTS, DIGITAL TEXTILE PRINTING **MATERIALS** RESIN, VARIOUS MATERIAL FINISHES, SILK **WEBSITE** JORGE-AYALA.COM / AYALAPARIS.COM

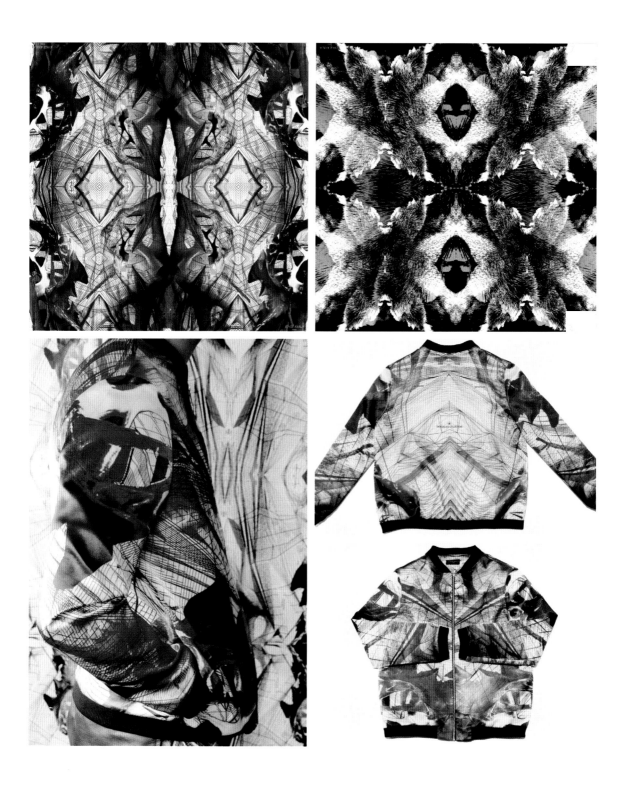

ABOVE
Transgressions pattern, from the *Clandestino* collection,
Spring/Summer 2015, digitally printed stretched cotton;
pictured in the Jorge Ayala Paris pop-up boutique,
September 2014

OPPOSITE
Supernatural Series pattern (top left and bottom), from
the *Stalking Architecture* collection, Autumn/Winter 2014,
digitally printed silk; *Synthetic Natures* pattern (top right),
from the *Clandestino* collection, Spring/Summer 2015,
digitally printed 250g polyester

'My works engage with a criticism of the
monochrome standardization we risk when we
take the digital for the sake of digital. Matter,
texture, structure, form and failure are all part
of the knowledge I am building through my
post-digital explorations.'

'I employ a varied armamentarium of technological tools to create sculptures that are completely different to those made by my historical forebears – to push my art in directions that would not otherwise be possible.'

BARRY X BALL

BREATHING LIFE INTO PORTRAITS OF STONE

In his endeavours to present a new type of sculptural portraiture, artist Barry X Ball celebrates the artisanship of sculptors from antiquity, while creating something equally revolutionary through the application of advanced digital technologies to the making of each of his works.

For *Envy* (these pages) and *Purity* (overleaf), Ball took as his starting point two sculptures from the permanent collection of Ca' Rezzonico in Venice: *Invidia* (*c*. 1670), by Giusto Le Court, and *Purità* (*c*. 1720–5), by Antonio Corradini. Beginning by 3D-scanning the marble busts to create a detailed mesh of data, he then re-sculpted the digital model, refining the unresolved details of the originals and rebuilding areas of historic damage, as well as making subtle changes to enhance their impact. Unlike their predecessors, Ball's works are created to be viewed from all angles, so the details – front and back – were perfected accordingly.

Once the digital models were complete, a series of the busts were carved from a variety of carefully selected, non-traditional stones. Ball used sophisticated CNC machines to start with, enabling the stone to be milled accurately from a variety of angles. The carving process was then finished with extensive hand-detailing and selective polishing, which took up to two thousand hours for each sculpture. Most of the completed sculptures are mirror images of their historical inspirations – a common feature of Ball's work – a reference to the fact that each is a reinterpretation, or 'reflection', of its source.

LOCATION NEW YORK, USA **PROJECT** *ENVY* (2008–12) AND *PURITY* (2008–13) **TECHNIQUES** 3D-SCANNING, 3D-MODELLING SOFTWARE, CNC LATHE, HAND-POLISHING **MATERIALS** VARIOUS STONES **WEBSITE** BARRYXBALL.COM

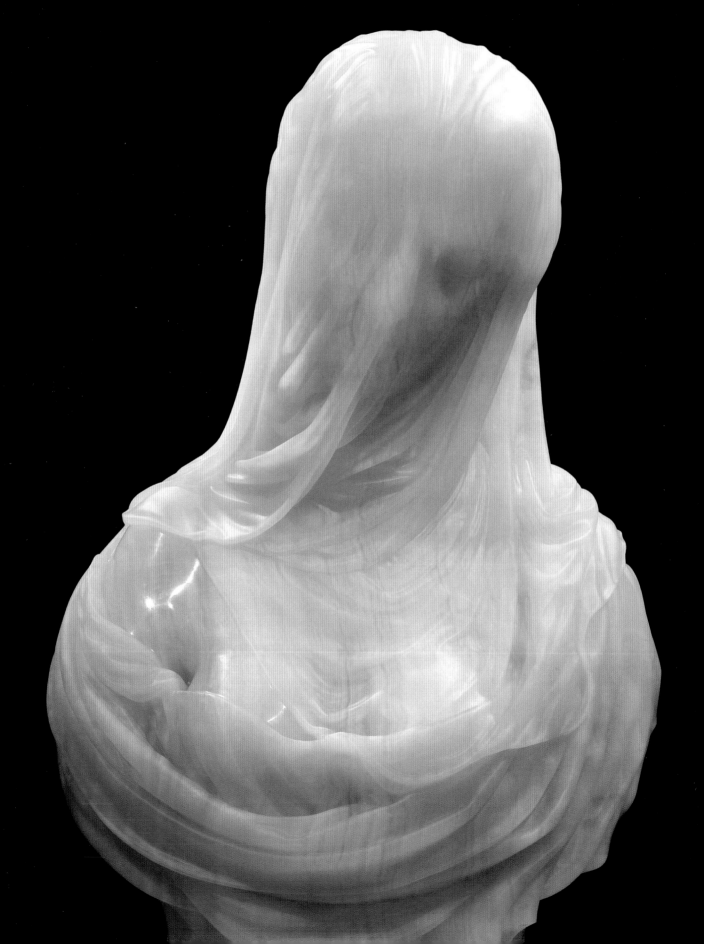

THESE PAGES
Purity, 2008–13, in Namibian sodalite (above)
and pink Iranian onyx (opposite), 61 cm (24 in.) high

ABOVE
La Ronde No. 2, 2011,
159 × 216 cm (63 × 85 in.), woven
on a warp with two threads (tencel
and stainless steel); mix of linen and
wool, with copper yarn; coloured dyes
applied to the woven surface

OPPOSITE
Compagnons No. 2, 2012,
168 × 244 cm (66 × 96 in.), woven on
a white warp using a black shuttle;
coloured dyes applied to the
woven surface

'Digital tools are the tools of today,
and bring more opportunities.
The digital preparation of files takes
less time, which forces me to be more
creative, to perfect the result, to
experiment with the yarns. There is
no excuse to feel limited.'

Internationally renowned for her explorations into Jacquard weaving
and digital embroidery, Canadian artist Louise Lemieux Bérubé creates
compelling textile artworks with a visual quality that meets somewhere
between photography and weaving.

She begins her designs by creating intricate collages of photographs
and drawings, then uses dedicated software to develop a highly detailed
weaving file, which transfers an incredible level of detail from the digital
artwork to the computerized loom. This process reduces the number
of colours in the image to match the number of threads possible in the
weave structure. The translation also determines the dimensions for the
artwork; each pixel in the image represents one thread on the loom.

Bérubé weaves in both colour (up to twenty-six colours of thread)
and monochrome (with black and white threads creating around thirteen
shades of grey), and chooses a time-intensive weaving process that
is part automated and part manual, allowing her to vary the yarn
materials as she works, to create different visual effects.

For her digitally embroidered artworks, Bérubé creates a machine
file using dedicated software, which assigns colours by layers in a
similar way to printing. Each colour in the image will necessitate a
corresponding spool of a single colour or blend of threads. Once the
textile production is complete, she then finishes each artwork with
additional hand-embroidery or the application of dyes to the surface.

LOUISE LEMIEUX BÉRUBÉ

FINDING A PLACE BETWEEN PHOTOGRAPHY AND WEAVING

LOCATION MONTREAL, CANADA **TECHNIQUES** POINTCARRÉ
WEAVING SOFTWARE, EMBIRD EMBROIDERY SOFTWARE, MANUAL
JACQUARD WEAVING, DIGITAL EMBROIDERY, HAND-EMBROIDERY,
HAND-DYEING **WEBSITE** LEMIEUXBERUBE.COM

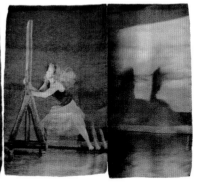

ABOVE

74 Directions, 2010, 140 × 518 cm (55 × 204 in.), woven on a warp with two types of threads (tencel and stainless steel); mix of linen and wool, with copper yarn added; yellow dyes applied to the woven surface

OPPOSITE

Rodin et Claudel No. 1 (top), 2012, 244 × 412 cm (96 × 162 in.), and *Rodin et Claudel No. 2* (bottom), 2012, 183 × 290 cm (72 × 114 in.), woven on a white warp using a black shuttle; coloured dyes applied to the woven surface

TOP

Joe No. 3 (left), 2012, 168 × 108 cm (66 × 43 in.), woven on a white warp using a black shuttle; coloured dyes applied to the woven surface; *Co-ex Cathédrale* (right), 2008, 170 × 108 cm (67 × 43 in.), woven on a white warp using a black shuttle and a blue shuttle, alternated to create the blue and grey shades

ABOVE
Swarovski crystals on the
gown's shoulder (top); dusting
off a shoulder piece in the
sintering tank (bottom)

OPPOSITE
Dita Von Teese, modelling
her fully articulated
3D-printed gown

FRANCIS BITONTI

EMBRACING THE VERNACULAR OF THE FUTURE

Architect and designer Francis Bitonti believes that if we are to design for the future, we must embrace its vernacular. To this end, his studio is deeply invested in researching the limits of emerging manufacturing technologies.

In 2013, Bitonti hit the headlines with his 3D-printed gown for burlesque artist and style icon Dita Von Teese, created in collaboration with costume designer Michael Schmidt. The fully articulated garment was informed by the geometry of the Golden Ratio – used in the mathematics of architecture and found in the structure of natural forms – which resulted in a spiralling, netted form that allows the wearer to move freely.

Using various CAD-modelling software packages, Bitonti detailed 2,633 independent links to build up the mesh silhouette – the completed model was then split into seventeen individual parts in order to manufacture the complex curved forms. Each piece of the dress was laser-sintered in white nylon, before being hand-assembled and stitched to create the final garment, which was dyed black and embellished with thousands of Swarovski crystals.

LOCATION NEW YORK, USA **PROJECT** *DITA'S GOWN* (2013)
TECHNIQUES CAD-MODELLING, LASER-SINTERING, HAND-EMBELLISHING **MATERIALS** POLYAMIDE NYLON, CRYSTALS
WEBSITE FRANCISBITONTI.COM

'The accessibility of new technologies for the creative process is resulting in designers becoming freed from the restrictions of their materials – they are no longer limited by their knowledge of how a material must behave, or what they can physically model.'

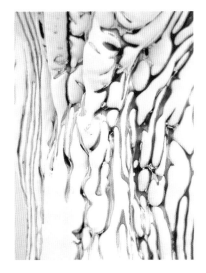

THESE PAGES
Pi][ar, 2014, ceramic
and 18-carat gold

ISAÏE BLOCH

CONCEIVED FROM NATURAL FORM AND DIGITAL LOGIC

Combining the disciplines of architecture, sculpture, design, fashion and fine art in his work, Isaïe Bloch contrasts the decadence of Baroque and Renaissance ornament with cutting-edge digital manufacturing techniques to create an other-worldly aesthetic, trapped somewhere between natural form and digital logic. He believes that none of this work could have been created without the capabilities of 3D-printing.

Cutlery Set (pp. 34, 35) showcases Bloch's ability to manipulate technological processes to create objects that appear crafted from organic material in the process of decomposition. Each piece was sculpted in CAD, and models 3D-printed in wax prior to casting the final versions in sterling silver and 18-carat gold-plated brass. Inspired by the decadent aesthetic of Romanticism, the *Floralia* vase (p. 35) progresses the style to show the scope of Bloch's advanced material manipulations. It is crafted from 3D-printed synthetic sandstone, a composite of fine gypsum-based powder, coloured inks and a resin binder.

The *Chroma* range of milk jugs (p. 34) combines rapid-prototyping techniques with an internal laser-sintered polyamide canister and 3D-printed ceramic detailing. A recent work, *Pi][ar* (these pages), is an exploration into the classical orders of columns, subverting the traditional construction process, topological characteristics and symmetrical logic. Modelled in CAD and CNC-milled, the resulting structures demonstrate a fabrication process of subtracting material, rather than building volume.

LOCATION GHENT, BELGIUM **TECHNIQUES** CAD-MODELLING, 3D-PRINTING, LOST-WAX CASTING, CNC-MILLING **MATERIALS** CERAMIC, SILVER, BRASS, 18-CARAT GOLD, SYNTHETIC SANDSTONE **WEBSITE** ERAGATORY.BLOGSPOT.CO.UK

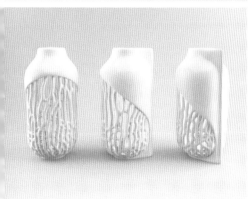

ABOVE
Cutlery Set (top left), 2011, 18-carat gold-plated brass and 925 sterling silver; *Chroma* (bottom left and right), 2013, ceramic

'At present, the enterprise of craft and design is in a state of flux, evolving through processes of adjustment and mutation. But we need to ask ourselves how we can augment custom character within digitally fabricated products. We should seek to use specific manufacturing and material misfits as a design opportunity.'

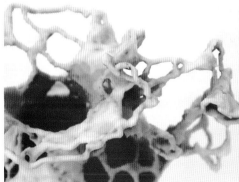

ABOVE
Cutlery Set (left), 2011, 18-carat gold-plated brass and 925 sterling silver; *Floralia* (top and bottom), 2012, 3D-printed sandstone, 9.5 × 18 × 14 cm (4 × 7 × 6 in.)

ICON

'I was looking for a way to link decoration and technology, to create something that was not nostalgic. I realized by using this process it was possible to create something that would be impossible to make by hand, and therefore could not have existed in the past.'

THESE PAGES
Garland Light, 2002, in silver (above) and brass (opposite)

TORD BOONTJE

THE HIGH-TECH ESSENCE OF NATURAL FORMS

Product designer Tord Boontje's *Garland Light* for Habitat is a highly successful example of combining craftsmanship with computer-aided manufacturing in a way that creates a mass-consumable piece of beautiful design.

Conceived in 2002 as part of his ongoing explorations into the potential of combining and contrasting natural forms with cutting-edge digital technology, this intricate tangle of flowers and leaves became an early icon for a new era of consumer products. It was first exhibited by the British Council, and can now be found in over half a million homes worldwide.

The computer-designed garland pattern is cut into paper-thin sheets of silver, copper or brass, using the technique of photochemical etching (commonly used for making tiny components for circuit boards). This process enables a far greater level of precision than would otherwise have been achievable if cutting by hand or even with a laser.

LOCATION LONDON, UK **PROJECT** *GARLAND LIGHT* (2002)
TECHNIQUES GRAPHIC SOFTWARE, PHOTOCHEMICAL ETCHING
MATERIALS SILVER, COPPER, BRASS SHEETS
WEBSITE TORDBOONTJE.COM

VALISSA
BUTTERWORTH

CELEBRATING THE MARKS
OF MACHINE AND HAND

Ceramicist Valissa Butterworth's *Pieces of Porcelain* collection is an evolving series of fine ceramics produced through the fusion of cutting-edge technologies and traditional techniques. When designing the series, Butterworth drew inspiration from the artisans of past centuries across the sectors of jewelry, ceramics and glass.

Starting with a simple vessel, each design is developed in CAD, with a carefully modelled textural tile applied across the surface. A prototype of the complete object is then 3D-printed in resin-bonded plaster, using the additive layer manufacturing technique. From this model, casting moulds are made in silicone and then in plaster. If the object is too large for 3D-printing, the prototype model is carved from Ureol, a tooling board, using five-axis CNC-milling machines. The final pieces are slip-cast by hand, using coloured Limoges porcelain to give a rich, bold colour.

Butterworth chooses to retain the marks of the making process: the textures on the external surfaces record signs of the printing and milling technologies used, while the internal surfaces have been smoothed by hand. Some pieces feature coloured glazes to enhance the textures and further celebrate the fusion of technology and craft. She uses a similar methodology in her lighting range, 3D-printing and then casting the white lampshades in plain porcelain. For the glass versions of her lamps, a mould in plaster or wood is carved using five-axis CNC-milling, or shaped from machined aluminium with hinges, into which coloured glass is blown.

OPPOSITE
Pieces of Porcelain, 2013,
Limoges porcelain in
various colours

LOCATION MELBOURNE, AUSTRALIA **TECHNIQUES** CAD-MODELLING, 3D-PRINTING, MOULD-MAKING, SLIP-CASTING, GLAZING **MATERIALS** LIMOGES PORCELAIN, GLASS **WEBSITE** THEMODCOLLECTIVE.COM.AU

ABOVE
Marquise lampshade, glass

OPPOSITE
Patterns including *Marquise* (top, middle left
and bottom right), *Bloom* (middle right)
and *Diamond* (bottom left)

'The relentless march of technology has
created an entirely new concept for the
traditional artisan. We live in the twenty-first
century and I believe we should embrace the
tools available to us, use them to take our
craft beyond the traditional and create
the extraordinary.'

EMILY COBB

FANTASTICAL FAIRY TALES IN CONTEMPORARY TECHNOLOGIES

'I approach digital technologies as an artistic medium, defined by the materials, as well as the methods of production. This approach always pushes me to think of more innovative uses, instead of just making pre-existing processes easier or faster.'

Jewelry designer Emily Cobb explores the potential of digital modelling and 3D-printing as part of the artisanal process. *Miss Madame's Magical-Grow* (p. 44) headpiece and rings represents her first transition to digital techniques. In this piece, the mice – which grow out of the hand-sculpted steel sheet flowers – were CAD-modelled and 3D-printed in simple nylon. The prints were then used as models to create silicone moulds, from which the final mouse-shapes were cast in flexible white resin.

The Elk with Antlers That Never Stopped Growing (opposite) was digitally sculpted before the separate elements – over fifty – were 3D-printed in nylon. Cobb then hand-painted or dyed each one before assembling the complete headpiece. A similar approach was used for *Billy's Bubble Blower* (p. 44), a neck accessory combining a sterling-silver bubble blower with a translucent photopolymer bubble containing a goldfish. The bubble was 3D-modelled and printed in two parts, before being sanded and polished to increase transparency. The goldfish, also printed in nylon, was hand-dyed before being inserted into the bubble.

Wanting to create a 3D-printed accessory that felt as flexible as fabric, Cobb created the *Constrictor* glove (p. 45), which features a tiny ball-and-socket lace formation that can be printed in sheets. By cutting the sheets in a flat pattern, rearranging and snapping the joints together, she was able to create the hand with no stitching or seams, before attaching it to the 3D-printed jaws of the 'snake', which is wrapped around the wearer's arm. For *Ursula's Envy: The Seahorse and the Violin* (p. 45), Cobb designed a mechanism of minute 3D-printed pegs, which wearers use to fasten, or 'tune', the photopolymer brooch onto their clothing.

LOCATION PHILADELPHIA, PENNSYLVANIA, USA
TECHNIQUES METALSMITHING, CAD-MODELLING, 3D-PRINTING, LOST-WAX CASTING, PAINTING **MATERIALS** STERLING SILVER, RESIN, PHOTOPOLYMER **WEBSITE** EMILY-COBB.COM

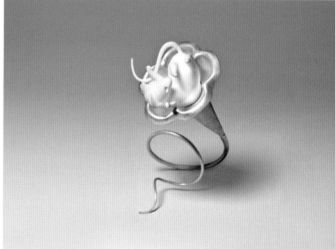

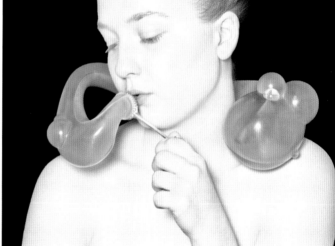

ABOVE
Become Undone: The Dove, 2013,
neckpiece in nylon and
sterling silver

TOP
Miss Madame's Magical-Grow, 2010,
headpiece in resin, sterling silver
and cubic zirconia

BOTTOM
Billy's Bubble Blower, 2011, neckpiece
in photopolymer and sterling silver

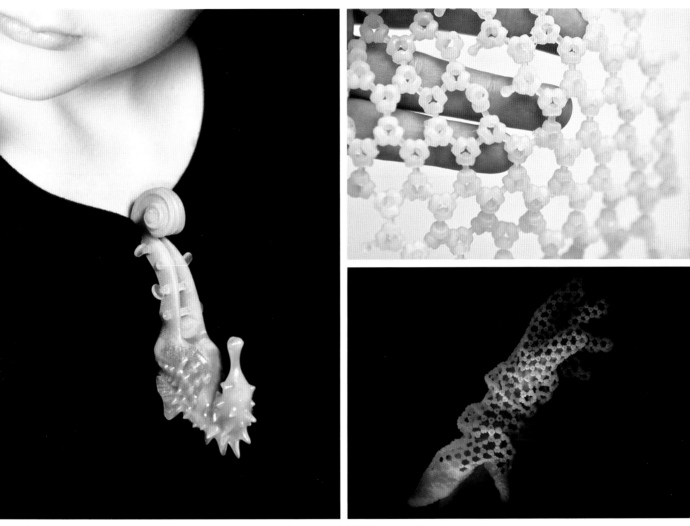

ABOVE
Ursula's Envy: The Seahorse and the Violin, 2011,
brooch in photopolymer

TOP AND BOTTOM
Constrictor, 2012, glove in photopolymer

LIA COOK

'Digital tools have brought an immediacy and flexibility to my work, allowing me to translate images through weaving in ways I would otherwise never have been able to conceive. I can continue to be innovative in the technical realm, as well as the artistic.'

OPPOSITE
Inner Tracts, 2014, cotton and rayon

In her work, artist Lia Cook studies the relationship between photographic portraiture and the sensuous, tactile nature of textiles. All of her pieces are produced on a digital hand loom, through which the pixels of a digital image are translated into interlacing threads.

Exploring a viewer's natural and powerful desire to reach out and touch the face of a woven portrait, much of Cook's recent work features woven translations of photographic portraits overlaid with images of neural pathways, created in collaboration with neuroscientists. *Intensity Su Data* (p. 49) captures the brain data associated with the intensity rating of a viewer's desire to touch the face depicted – first looking at a photograph, and then the woven translation. In another project, *Connectome*, a portrait is superimposed with diffusion spectrum imaging patterns of the neural connections within the white matter of the brain – patterns that, in themselves, also appear woven.

Cook's early work *Iterations,* a series of six pieces featuring the same doll face, is a study of how the small changes in the way an image is translated by the weaving process can alter the emotional impact of each image and the expression of the subject. The evolving *Su Series* (p. 48) – featuring the same portrait of a child as the starting point for each piece – is a further exploration into the effect of varying translation techniques during the weaving process. This ongoing study currently consists of fifteen pieces, and will eventually grow to cover a whole gallery wall.

LOCATION BERKELEY, CALIFORNIA, USA **TECHNIQUES** DIGITAL IMAGING, WEAVING ON DIGITAL HAND LOOM **MATERIALS** COTTON, RAYON **WEBSITE** LIACOOK.COM

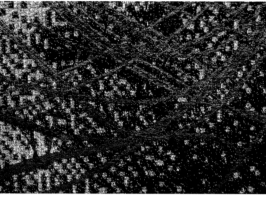

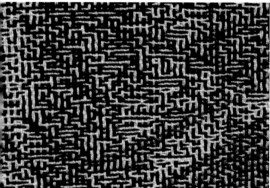

ABOVE
Su Series, 2008, cotton and rayon

OPPOSITE
Clockwise from top:
Facing Touch, 2011; *Doll Face V*, 2009;
Intensity Su Data, 2013, cotton and rayon

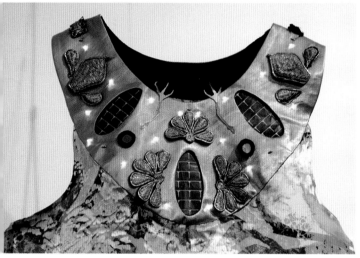

ABOVE
Solar Vintage, 2009,
clockwise from top left: Illuminated
lace necklace; solar fan; embroidered
parasol; illuminated cocktail dress

OPPOSITE
Embroidered parasol,
from *Solar Vintage*, 2009

'Any tools are extensions of our mind
and body, allowing our imagination
to be materialized. It is a natural step
in the current technological evolution
to use digital tools as a means to
an end. What it is more interesting
is how the nature of those means
actually modify the results in ways
we could not have predicted.'

In a marketplace obsessed with the concept of 'wearable technology',
ecologically minded researcher and designer Elena Corchero creates
beautiful accessories with a unique twist, combining technology
with the craft aesthetic and skills of haute-couture fashion.

Alongside lines of health-aware jewelry and street-safe reflective
knitwear, Corchero's *Solar Vintage* collection explores delicate ways
of integrating organic solar cells into beautiful one-off textile pieces,
to create ornate, embellished accessories such as fans, parasols and
necklaces. The solar cells, featured in the decorative embellishments
of each piece, are as flexible and lightweight as a textile, and store up
energy while being worn or carried outdoors during the day. These
objects take on a dual life by turning into home accessories by night,
emitting decorative ambient light from small LEDs integrated into
the embellished surface of each piece.

Along with vintage textiles, each piece includes refined, digitally
made lace designs and smart textile weaves that integrate conductive
threads, enabling the direct transfer of energy from the organic solar cell
to LEDs through the fabric itself. As photovoltaic technology develops,
future versions of these accessories may be able to charge a range
of portable devices, including mobile phones, music players
and cameras.

ELENA CORCHERO

WHERE TECHNOLOGY MEETS THE TRADITIONS OF HAUTE-COUTURE CRAFT

LOCATION LONDON, UK **TECHNIQUES** DIGITAL PATTERN DESIGN, DIGITAL KNITTING, DIGITAL LACE-MAKING, EMBROIDERY **MATERIALS** CONDUCTIVE THREADS, VINTAGE TEXTILES, WOOD AND CELLULOSE-BASED MATERIALS, ELECTRONICS AND ORNATE CIRCUIT BOARDS, ORGANIC SOLAR CELLS **WEBSITE** ELENACORCHERO.COM

'When dreaming up new designs,
what excites me most is to create
new functionalities, and make things
possible that were not possible before –
no matter how small.'

MICHIEL CORNELISSEN

THE LIMITLESS POTENTIAL OF SMALL OBJECTS

ABOVE
Mesh Matryoshkas, 3D-printed
earrings and pendants

OPPOSITE
Clockwise from top left:
Mesh Matryoshkas; *Merry
Bird*, pendant in laser-sintered
polyamide nylon; *KXX*,
3D-printed rattling rings; *One
in a Million Bird*, algorithm-
generated, individually printed
polyamide nylon rings

Combining his industrial design expertise with an interest in the potential
of digital manufacturing, Michiel Cornelissen's small, collectible designs
are explorations of objects that are as limitless in structural possibility as
the software that sculpts them. His ultimate exploration to date has been
the *One in a Million Bird* (opposite, bottom left), a series of one million
unique rings, each with a bird that is slightly different from the next and
numbered accordingly. The algorithm-generated rings are 'grown' to
order, splicing a combination of body type and posture. The rings are
then laser-sintered in polyamide for a durable, high-quality finish.

An earlier work, *Merry Bird* (opposite, top right), led to the creation of
the finely crafted *Mesh Matryoshkas* jewelry series (above and opposite,
top left), which takes the form of the Russian doll and turns it into a
tiny vehicle for exploring the level of detail and complexity of formation
achievable through laser-sintered production. The nesting shapes and
lattices are created as one object at the moment of manufacture.

And, pushing the medium further, Cornelissen's *KXX* rings (opposite,
bottom right), created to celebrate the 2014 World Cup in Brazil, takes
the form of a tiny version of the *caxixi*, an Afro-Brazilian percussion
instrument, with beads inside the head of the ring that rattle when
shaken. The tiny beads were created in situ and fused in polyamide as
part of the one-piece manufacturing process, rather than being inserted
after assembly, as with traditional versions of the instrument.

LOCATION ANTWERP, BELGIUM **TECHNIQUES** 3D SOFTWARE,
LASER-SINTERING **MATERIALS** POLYAMIDE NYLON
WEBSITE MICHIELCORNELISSEN.COM

'I have used CAD for years, but there always needed to be an element of translation through traditional prototyping and production. Direct digital manufacturing has brought the final artefacts that much closer to the forms in my imagination.'

LIONEL T. DEAN

TRADITION MEETS KITSCH THROUGH NEW TECHNOLOGIES

OPPOSITE
Fabergé, 2013,
3D-printed sculpture,
15 × 27 cm (6 × 11 in.)

Lionel T. Dean has worked at the forefront of research into the creative potential and flexibility of direct digital manufacturing for over a decade. His exceptionally intricate work, *Fabergé* (these pages), is an homage to the precious eggs produced by the Fabergé jewelry firm and is offered as an ornament for the post-industrial era. As with those before it, the decorative elements of the work represent the preoccupations of our age – wealth, power, success and optimism – as well as demonstrate exceptional craftsmanship.

The egg features approximately one hundred pieces of 3D iconography, none of which are necessarily precious or symbolic, but representative of our commercial world. Each was individually modelled in CAD, before being intertwined into one whole digital model. The complete, complex form was then produced by selective laser-sintering in polyamide, produced in two halves – a top and a bottom – then hand-painted with realistic, original detail to complete the work.

LOCATION LEICESTER, UK **PROJECT** *FABERGÉ* (2013)
TECHNIQUES CAD-MODELLING, SELECTIVE LASER-SINTERING,
HAND-PAINTING **MATERIALS** POLYAMIDE NYLON
WEBSITE FUTUREFACTORIES.COM

WIM DELVOYE

CLASSICAL SCULPTURE WITH AN INDUSTRIAL TWIST

'Rarely does a good idea come from a digital tool. And most artists define themselves before they start, which also limits these ideas. Better to have an idea and then define the tool required, then there is no difference between artisanal tools and digital ones.'

Belgian artist Wim Delvoye's body of work demonstrates a radical approach to the use of industrial processes in contemporary art, and combines some of the oldest and the newest production techniques in the formation of his compelling, other-worldly sculptures.

For the ongoing *Bronzes* series of Rorschach-inspired pieces, Delvoye begins by 3D-scanning an antique sculpture, and then manipulating the digitized form using his trademark twisting and morphing techniques. The resulting form is then 3D-printed in resin. The size of the printed pieces is limited by the machinery, so each sculpture is divided into a number of sections for printing (it would be impossible to cast some of the more twisted sculptures as whole objects, owing to the complexity of the structure). Moulds are then created from the separate pieces, which are cast in bronze using the lost-wax method, before being welded together. Finally, the sculptures are polished to a high shine.

For his *Gothic* series, Delvoye designs each sculpture using CAD software, again applying his twisting and slanting treatments to the digital model. Each sculpture designed in this way requires hundreds of hours at the screen, and tens of thousands of mouse-clicks. Once the form and detailing are perfected, the individual flat plates are laser-cut from thin steel sheets. For a piece such as *Twisted Dump Truck* (p. 59), 2,450 separate plates are welded together to form the final sculpture, which is then sand-blasted, polished or nickel-plated to finish.

OPPOSITE
Nautilus, 2012, from the *Gothic* series, laser-cut stainless steel, 103 × 97.5 × 50 cm (41 × 38 × 20 in.)

LOCATION GHENT, BELGIUM **TECHNIQUES** CAD SOFTWARE, LASER-CUTTING, 3D-PRINTING, BRONZE CASTING **MATERIALS** RESIN, BRONZE, STAINLESS STEEL **WEBSITE** WIMDELVOYE.BE

ABOVE LEFT
Le Secret, 2011, polished bronze
64 × 25 × 26 cm (25 x 10 x 10 in.)

ABOVE RIGHT
Amor Rorschach, 2012, nickelled bronze
41 × 17.5 × 30.8 cm (16 × 7 × 12 in.)

RIGHT
Trinity Rorschach, 2012, nickelled bronze
33.5 × 32 × 30 cm (13 × 13 × 12 in.)

OPPOSITE
Twisted Dump Truck, 2011, laser-cut stainless steel,
75 × 200 × 80 cm (30 × 79 × 31 in.)

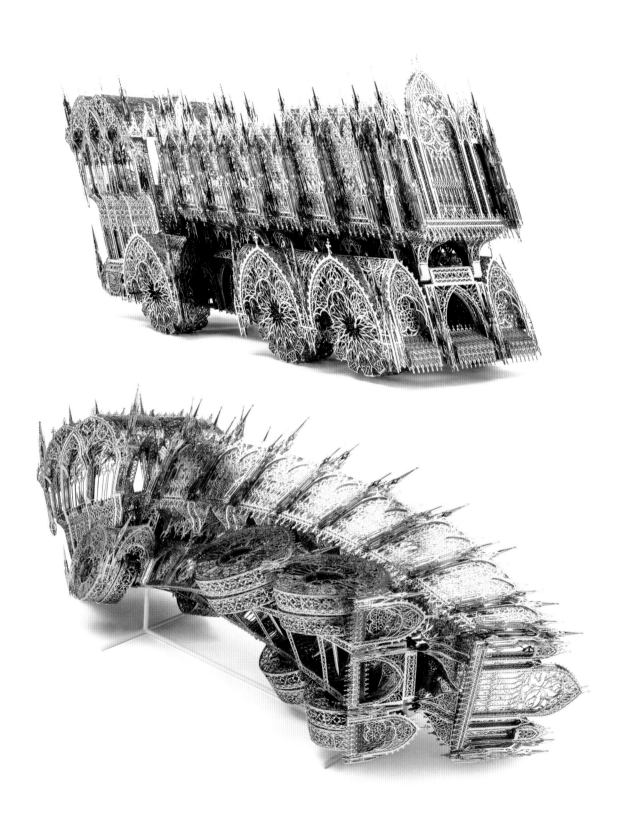

OLAF DIEGEL

THE FREEDOM OF CUSTOMIZATION IN INSTRUMENTAL FORM

'Digital and handcraft tools can work together in great harmony. With my guitars, the 3D-printing process allows me to make the otherwise impossible bodies, while the necks are crafted out of wood and the assembly is very much a process of touch and feel. It's the best of both worlds.'

ABOVE
Americana, mahogany inner core, maple neck with rosewood fret board, Corian nut, chrome hardware. Airbrushed eagle's head by Ron van Dam

OPPOSITE
Steampunk, maple inner core and neck with maple fret board, Corian nut, chrome hardware. Airbrushed detailing by Ron van Dam

An experienced design engineer, Olaf Diegel launched ODD Guitars to explore the limits of digitally assisted manufacturing. Initially designed and modelled in CAD, each guitar is made to order, based on a series of style options. The production process involves a combination of rapid-prototyping, CNC-milling and hand-finishing and decoration, with the final addition of top-quality hardware. The bodies are printed using the selective laser-sintering process in white polyamide. The build up of the 3D-print of each body takes approximately eleven hours and, once completed, each is dyed or hand-painted and decorated.

Designs such as *Scarab* (p. 62) and *Spider* (p. 63) demonstrate body structures that are formulated specifically for selective laser-sintered production, created as single components that could not be manufactured any other way. For the iconic *Steampunk* model (opposite), the entire body, including the moving gears and pistons, is fabricated as a single piece, with no further assembly required. All of the guitars feature a wooden inner core, neck and fret board – made from mahogany, maple or rosewood – which are carved to order using CNC-milling tools, before being finished by hand, including hammering the frets and inserting mother-of-pearl inlays. The final touch is the laser-cut ODD logo, in a contrasting colour of veneer, which is inlaid into the neck of the guitar.

Diegel has recently expanded his explorations into 3D-printed drum kits and electric keyboard detailing.

LOCATION LUND, SWEDEN **TECHNIQUES** CAD SOFTWARE, SELECTIVE LASER-SINTERING, CNC-MILLING **MATERIALS** POLYAMIDE NYLON, VARIOUS WOODS, WOOD VENEERS **WEBSITE** ODD.ORG.NZ

ABOVE
Dark Red Atom, custom-dyed and lacquered nylon body, mahogany inner core, maple neck and fret board, Corian nut, gold hardware

ABOVE, MIDDLE AND RIGHT
Scarab, dyed and lacquered nylon webbed structure, mahogany inner core, maple neck with rosewood fret board, mother-of-pearl inlay, Corian nut, chrome hardware

OPPOSITE, TOP LEFT
Blue Atom, custom-dyed and lacquered nylon body, mahogany inner core, maple neck and fret board, Corian nut, chrome hardware

OPPOSITE, TOP RIGHT AND BOTTOM RIGHT
Hive Bass, painted and lacquered nylon hexagonal structure, maple inner core, maple neck with rosewood fret board, Corian nut, black hardware

OPPOSITE, BOTTOM LEFT
Spider, dyed and lacquered nylon webbed structure, mahogany inner core, maple neck with rosewood fret board, mother-of-pearl inlay, Corian nut, chrome hardware

DAVID
D'IMPERIO

THE FUSING OF OLD-SCHOOL HANDCRAFT AND MECHANICAL PRECISION

'My work celebrates the beauty of arbitrary geometric tendencies that occur in the natural world. To really explore the properties of these forms it is important to me to first work by hand, but I fuse these old-school methods with efficient fabrication technologies for precise translation of my designs into finished pieces.'

OPPOSITE
Atlas (top) and *Beeline* (bottom), linear-suspension lamps, laser-cut stainless steel

Artist David D'Imperio designs and builds lighting designs that are as much sculptural art forms as they are functional furnishings. Each has a lightweight aluminium interior structure, encased in a stainless-steel statement facing. He typically begins each design with a pencil, paper and scissors, gradually shaping the design in three dimensions. Working with paper is important to the process, allowing D'Imperio to understand the properties of the thin, malleable sheets of steel with which he will later create the final piece.

For the *Atlas* linear-suspension design (opposite, top), derived from imagery of Rorschach inkblots, D'Imperio used flat sheets of tracing paper to find the most effective combination of inkblot shape, symmetry and layering, structural integrity and light penetration. Piecing together a series of inkblots into a linear formation, the resulting pattern resembles a topographic map. He then made a full-scale drawing of the design, playing with scale against other pieces of furniture to determine the perfect dimensions. The drawing was then scanned and converted into a digital file, and used as a template for laser-cutting the pattern from thin sheets of stainless steel. Each light is assembled by hand, twisting and folding the cut surfaces to create the final, three-dimensional form.

All of D'Imperio's designs follow a similar handcrafted process combined with machine fabrication, with some variations in assembly for each piece. For *Beeline* (opposite, bottom), the concept was to create a plane of shimmering facets, which resulted in the artist placing and rotating each hexagon individually on three different axes, based on a laser-cut 'hinge' design that was first perfected on paper.

LOCATION STONY RUN, PENNSYLVANIA, USA **TECHNIQUES** HAND-SCULPTING, CAD-DRAWING, LASER-CUTTING **MATERIALS** PAPER, STAINLESS STEEL, ALUMINIUM **WEBSITE** DAVIDDIMPERIO.COM

MICHAEL
EDEN

FREEING THE MAKING PROCESS
FROM THE POTTER'S WHEEL

Michael Eden practiced as a craft potter for over twenty years, creating traditional slip-decorated earthenware, before his experiments with rapid-prototyping technologies brought about a revolution in his work. Exploring the transition from hand to digital skills and the amalgamation of the two processes, he developed a signature style using computer modelling and selective laser-sintering in polyamide nylon. Each piece is hand-finished with non-fired, coloured ceramic coatings and a resin topcoat.

One of the first fully realized works to result from this new working method was the *Wedgwoodn't Tureen* (opposite, bottom left). In Eden's hands, this iconic form of eighteenth-century porcelain is re-imagined and instilled with a new significance, resulting in an object that could not have been made with conventional hand- or industrial ceramic processes. The bold coatings of the finished series consciously avoid the colour limitations and traditions of conventional glazes, and the tureen now stands as a modern representation of a new form of craftsmanship, 250 years after Josiah Wedgwood first pioneered his own industrial revolution in ceramic manufacture.

Eden continues to explore the potential of digital tools and reverse engineering, creating 3D captures of existing objects for manipulation, and devising extraordinary forms that integrate contemporary elements of communication – including barcodes and the pixellated aesthetic of digital symbols – in place of traditional techniques of surface decoration.

LOCATION MILNTHORPE, CUMBRIA, UK **TECHNIQUES** CAD SOFTWARE,
SELECTIVE LASER-SINTERING, HAND-FINISHING **MATERIALS** POLYAMIDE
NYLON, CERAMIC COATINGS AND GLAZES **WEBSITE** MICHAEL-EDEN.COM

'I realized these technologies had the potential to free my creative process from the constraints of design for manufacture, and to free the making process from the centrifugal forces and gravity of the potter's wheel.'

ABOVE
The Mnemosyne, 2011, Carnegie Museum of Art, Pittsburgh, Pennsylvania, USA

THESE PAGES
Shells, 2011–12, by Marc Quinn,
exhibited in Venice, 2013

FACTUM ARTE

NATURAL FORMS FUSED WITH ADVANCED ENGINEERING

Pioneering studio Factum Arte develops bespoke digital tools and software to 'mediate' across the previously separate worlds of technology and craft skills. It is renowned for its creative partnerships with artists including Grayson Perry and Anish Kapoor, as well as Marc Quinn, for whom it produced the sculpture series, *Shells* (these pages).

The exterior surfaces of a group of shells, chosen from the collection of the Natural History Museum, London, were 3D-scanned using a Nub3D Triple scanning system. The resulting surface data was combined with cross-sectional scans of the interiors to create a three-dimensional model of each shell, which could then be structurally enlarged; the largest shell produced was 5m (16 ft) in length. The surface detailing of the shells was painstakingly rendered to ensure a close correspondence between form and scan throughout the digital translation process, and each shell carefully modified so that only three points touch the ground.

The digital models were then divided into pieces that could be stereo-lithographically printed in UV-cured resin, on a mammoth printer operated by Belgian firm Materialise. The printed pieces were then hand-assembled into a complete model, and the whole model again divided into sections. Silicone moulds were then made for the bronze-casting process, which used a mix of sand-casting and lost-wax technologies. The final bronze sections were welded together, ground down and chased to produce invisible joins. Once complete, the internal surfaces were mirror-polished, and the whole surface treated with an incralac varnish and microcrystalline wax to retain the bright colour of the bronze.

LOCATION MADRID, SPAIN **PROJECT** *SHELLS* (2011–12), BY MARC QUINN **TECHNIQUES** 3D-SCANNING, CAD-MODELLING, STEREOLITHOGRAPHY, BRONZE CASTING, HAND-FINISHING **MATERIALS** SLS RESIN, POLYURETHANE, SILICONE, BRONZE **WEBSITE** FACTUM-ARTE.COM

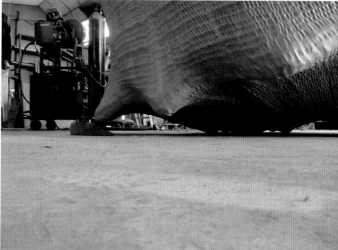

ABOVE LEFT
The assembled model, with printing artefacts removed to finish the surface

ABOVE RIGHT
Every shell is engineered so that only three points touch the ground

TOP LEFT
The shells are made from a mixture of data from an x-ray and structured-light scanning to create a naturally engineered form inside and out

TOP RIGHT
The interior surfaces of the finished shells are polished to a high shine, with the outer surfaces left textured to echo the natural form of a shell

'Digital information is essentially synaesthetic, and the emphasis is now on mediation and transformation – this conditions the diverse ways that ideas take shape and find their form.'

LEFT The bronze-cast sections are positioned and then welded, following the printed model and scan data

RIGHT The huge finished sculptures are transported on wheeled supporting frames

'We too easily rely on computers, even though they are very limited in their way of working. Our core idea is to use the limitations of a computer to make new shapes – and work to find the right techniques and the right methods. We experiment and ask a lot of questions.'

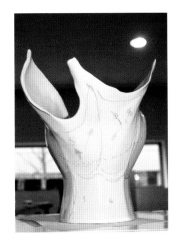

ABOVE
The cast porcelain vase,
before decoration

OPPOSITE
Digital models of five stages
during the process of
deforming the vase (top); the
final vase (bottom), cast in
porcelain with hand-painted
detailing that mirrors the
deformed pattern from the
surface of the digital model

FRONT

THE POWER OF THE WIND
IN VIRTUAL FORM

Design group Front conceives objects that communicate a story
to the observer about the design process, the material it is made
from and the conventions that are being disrupted.

For a ceramic commission for Moooi, the team began by
digitizing a classic Royal Blue Delft porcelain vase using a
3D-scanner, and converting it into a fully detailed CAD model,
complete with the original blue patterned surface detailing.
Utilizing software techniques commonly used for simulating the
effects of wind speed on architectural or automotive models,
the digital vase was then exposed to a big gust of virtual wind.

A version of the *Blown Away Vase* at its furthest reach was
fabricated using laser-sintered polyamide. A plaster mould was
then created from this prototype, so that Royal Delft could
produce a series of pieces in porcelain. Each vase was then
individually hand-decorated and finished by master painters,
mimicking every stretched detail of the original, digitally
deformed blue pattern.

LOCATION STOCKHOLM, SWEDEN **PROJECT** *BLOWN AWAY VASE*
(2008) **TECHNIQUES** CAD-MODELLING, LASER-SINTERING, PORCELAIN
MOULDING, HAND-PAINTING **MATERIALS** POLYAMIDE, PORCELAIN
WEBSITE DESIGNFRONT.ORG

As Designer-in-Residence at London's Design Museum in 2013, Adam Nathaniel Furman's response to the chosen theme of 'identity' was the creation of *Identity Parade*, a collection of curiosities that explores the combined potential of digital-fabrication technologies and traditional ceramic techniques.

Over the course of three months, Furman developed a series of objects that demonstrated how the accessibility of rapid-fabrication techniques frees designers from commercial parameters to create any number of objects with individual identities. Each object was conceived through a pairing of creative influence and output technique. He began each work by imagining a scenario for the design/maker (documented on his accompanying blog), bringing this together with fabrication techniques such as 3D-printed ceramic, sintered nylon or metal, or slip-cast porcelain developed from 3D-printed positives.

Initially, a digital version of the unique design was modelled, before it was physically fabricated using the designated technique. Some pieces were left as formed by a particular process, while others were finished traditionally with a range of slip glazes. This working methodology resulted in a large and eclectic array of designs – fifty-four pieces in total – each communicating a variation on the theme of the search for identity, which were exhibited together in the gallery as a dazzling demonstration of the potential of new and old craft techniques.

ADAM NATHANIEL FURMAN

UNBOUNDED POTENTIAL IN COMBINING TECHNOLOGY AND TRADITION

LOCATION LONDON, UK **TECHNIQUES** CAD-MODELLING, CERAMIC PRINTING, SELECTIVE LASER-SINTERING, SLIP-CASTING **MATERIALS** POLYAMIDE NYLON, CERAMIC, PORCELAIN, ALUMINIUM **WEBSITE** ADAMNATHANIELFURMAN.COM

'I believe that the more mediums an artist explores, the less our ideas are defined by any given process. So I think the more technology we use as artists, the more transparent our work becomes to the complexities of our creative explorations – leading to richer work and more unpredictable outcomes.'

THESE PAGES
The *Identity Parade* collection explored the combined potential of digital-fabrication technologies and traditional ceramics techniques

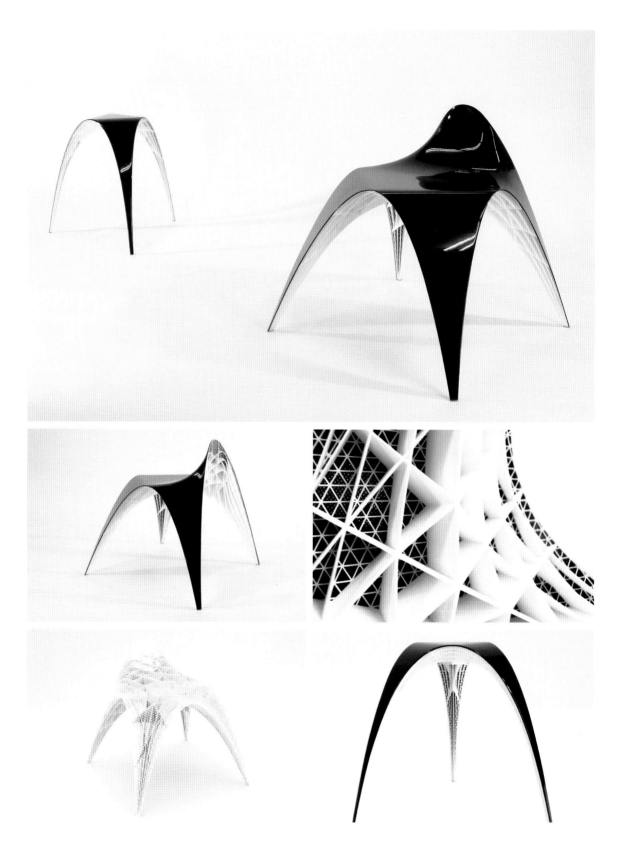

BRAM GEENEN

AN HISTORIC ARCHITECTURAL METHOD BROUGHT INTO THE FUTURE

'Technology isn't an end goal in itself, yet it can help achieve our ambitions. The same goes for craftsmanship; that too is a means to an end. When technology and craftsmanship work in parallel, both applied for their intrinsic strengths, then something special can be achieved.'

OPPOSITE
Gaudí Stool (top left), 2009, and *Gaudí Chair* (top right and middle left), 2011

Taking inspiration from the methods of the iconic Spanish architect Antoni Gaudí, Dutch designer Bram Geenen has created technically advanced furniture pieces that fuse organic lines with digital fabrication and the surface engineering seen in racing cars.

To establish the arched shape of the *Gaudí Chair* – an evolution of his earlier *Gaudí Stool* (both opposite) – models were created from chains that, suspended between two supports, fall naturally into parabolic curves. These catenary arches determine the strongest shapes for vertical structures; the technique was used by Gaudí to create buildings that were organic in form, but built according to the principles of nature to withstand gravitational forces. This basic shape was then turned into a digital model, to which forces were applied to simulate the weight subjected to it when a chair is sat on, dictating the shape of the ribs of the seat and back. The resulting design demonstrates the minimum volume of material required for maximum strength.

The materials and fabrication techniques used were chosen with the aim of achieving the complexity of the structure, while also creating an inherently strong yet lightweight object. The ribs were designed as one flowing form, from glass fibre-infused nylon, using the selective laser-sintering technique. Carbon fibre is used to make the smooth shell of the seat and back, chosen for its physical properties and because it allows the material to be shaped in double curves. To make the prototype chair, the carbon fibre was hand-laminated directly onto the 3D-printed substructure of ribs, in layers of carbon fabric and epoxy resin, which was then polished to a high shine. The later production batch of the chair was created using a mould and pre-impregnated resin sheets, to ensure even higher quality.

LOCATION AMSTERDAM, NETHERLANDS **PROJECT** *GAUDÍ STOOL* (2009) AND *GAUDÍ CHAIR* (2011) **TECHNIQUES** SUSPENDED CHAINS, CAD-MODELLING, SELECTIVE LASER-SINTERING, CARBON-FIBRE LAYERING **MATERIALS** GLASS FIBRE-INFUSED NYLON, CARBON FIBRE **WEBSITE** STUDIOGEENEN.COM

'The interface between life as it is lived and art through which life is represented is constantly being renegotiated, and digital technology is one of the most immediate and powerful imaging tools to be put into our hands. It allows us all to become participants in the representation of our lives, as well as in their transformation.'

ANTONY GORMLEY

A HUMAN MATRIX ON A MONUMENTAL SCALE

THESE PAGES AND OVERLEAF
Exposure, 2010.
The sculpture will evolve with the natural cycle of the land, gradually becoming buried in the built-up earth of the dyke as the sea level rises

Permanently installed on a dyke connecting the Dutch provinces of Friesland and Flevoland, 1 km (0.6 miles) from the shore, Antony Gormley's monumental *Exposure* is the artist's largest and most complex project to date. Standing 25m (82 ft) high and constructed from 5,000 individual struts, the crouching figure transforms Gormley's solid, sculptural language into an open, three-dimensional drawing.

The structure is a random matrix of mathematical ingenuity, with no defined load path or orthogonal logic. The use of bespoke CAD software enabled a refinement of a formation that would not otherwise have been possible, allowing the team to calculate the minimum material mass required to support such a scale and volume. The calculations are absolutely honed, each strut is necessary, its mass minimized: take one away, and the structure would no longer be sound.

The complex form evolved through physical and CAD models, created in collaboration with University College London, Cambridge University and design consultancy Royal Haskoning. A plaster cast of the artist was 3D-scanned to create a digitized model, which was then subjected to unique algorithms to define the dimensions and arrangement of the struts. The struts were hand-cut from galvanized steel, and fixed together in angle-sections that connect at 547 nodes, using a total of 14,000 bolts. The most congested nodes in the design correspond roughly to the chakras (energy points) of ancient Hindu thought.

The work was constructed in Scotland by the pylon manufacturers Had-Fab, alongside Dutch engineers, taking eighteen months to fabricate and install.

LOCATION UK **PROJECT** *EXPOSURE* (2010) **DIMENSIONS** 25.64 × 13.25 × 18.47 M (84 × 43 × 61 FT) **MATERIALS** GALVANIZED STEEL **WEBSITE** ANTONYGORMLEY.COM

ICON

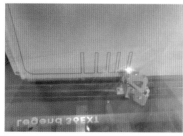

'I have always been intrigued by the way the whole chain of design, production and distribution of products works. And I always wondered if it would be possible to design a different system, facilitated by digital tools – so I went about inventing one.'

DAVID GRAAS

REIMAGINING THE PRODUCTION LINE OF TOMORROW

ABOVE
Graas's laser-cut furniture can be made from scrap corrugated cardboard boxes, giving each piece a unique character

OPPOSITE
Cardboard Lounge, 2009 (top left) and *Don't Spill Your Coffee*, 2007 (top right and bottom). Made from laser-cut cardboard panels, slotted together without the need for fixings or glue

The motivation behind the original designs for the *Don't Spill Your Coffee* table (opposite, top right and bottom) and the later *Cardboard Lounge* armchair (opposite, top left) was to carefully conceive smart pieces of furniture that could be made almost anywhere, efficiently, on demand.

An early pioneer of this growing movement, designer David Graas disengaged the design from the making of the object. By producing the design in a digital format, and using a widely available material, his furniture designs could, in theory, be cut by a workshop anywhere in the world and assembled by the customer.

Graas's concept was put into practice for an exhibition at the 2014 Edinburgh International Science Festival, for which the table was produced using discarded corrugated cardboard boxes from the local bike shop.

LOCATION HAARLEM, NETHERLANDS **PROJECT** *DON'T SPILL THE COFFEE* (2007) AND *CARDBOARD LOUNGE* (2009) **TECHNIQUES** CAD-MODELLING, LASER-CUTTING **MATERIALS** HEAVY-DUTY CORRUGATED CARDBOARD **WEBSITE** DAVIDGRAAS.COM

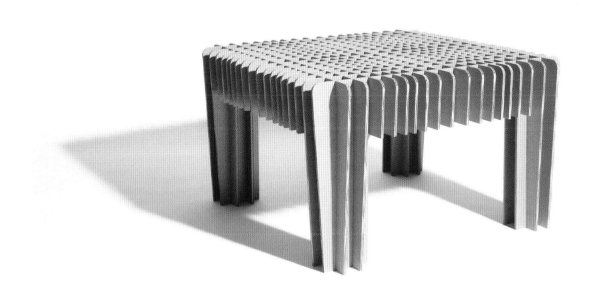

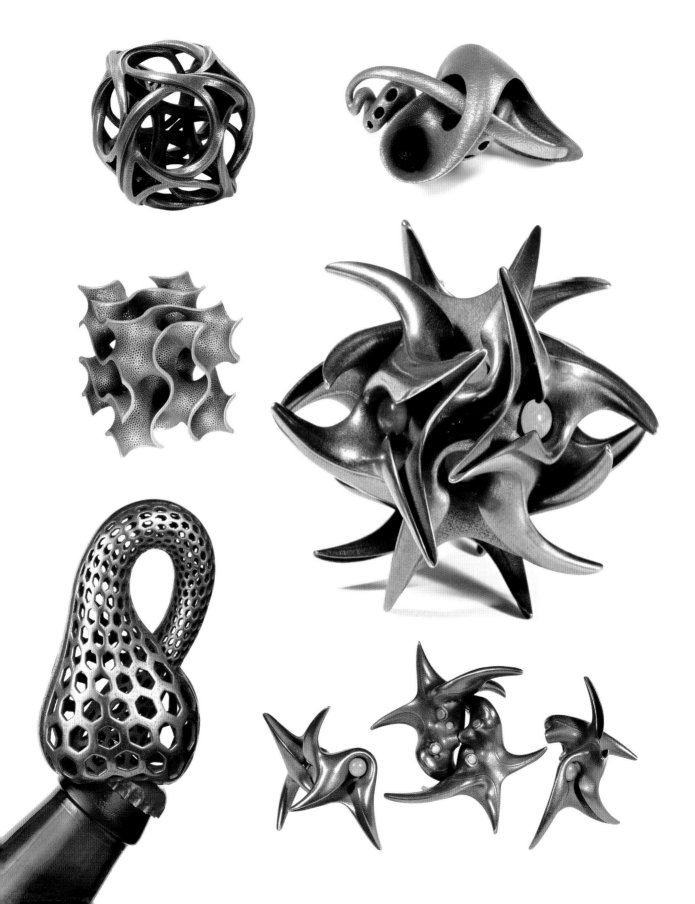

'In the beginning, I looked at an industrial injection-moulding technology and saw a new art medium. Through working with CAD/CAM software, suddenly the geometrical designs I saw in my mind's eye could be realized, and my coding skills became object-making ones.'

BATHSHEBA GROSSMAN

THE CRAFTED LANGUAGE OF MATHEMATICS IN SCULPTURAL FORM

ABOVE
Metatrino, 2003, with original digital rendering

OPPOSITE
Hyperwine, 2012 (top left), mathematical model; *Whelk*, 2010 (top right); *The Gyroid*, 2005 (middle left), mathematical model; *Ophan*, 2014 (middle right), assembled; *Klein Bottle Opener*, 2010 (bottom left), all sintered steel with bronze infiltration; *Ophan* (bottom right), disassembled

For over two decades, Bathsheba Grossman has pioneered the re-imagining of industrial 3D-printing technologies as new tools for the artist and craftsman. Her aesthetic focus has been fixed on exploring the potential of these tools in creating expressions of geometry in sculpture that would otherwise be impossible.

Devising intricate mathematical designs with BetaCAD software, Grossman initially used starch-based 3D-printing to make positives for lost-wax casting in bronze. The advent of direct metal printing revolutionized the process, immediately making her work more affordable and accessible to a wider audience of collectors. Grossman's method of free-form manufacturing has evolved to encompass collections of algorithmic, biomorphic and natural symmetrical formations, drawing on the structures of crystals, micro-organisms and simple invertebrates. She has become increasingly flexible with scale, creating large sculptural forms, as well as delicate smaller objects, which would have been impossible to conceive through any other medium.

Grossman's creative approach continues to challenge geometrical modelling and selective laser-sintering in metals, seeking to attain a beautiful simplicity and order in each design. By using the bare minimum of material structure, she is able to produce a strong mathematical sense of elegance.

LOCATION SOMERVILLE, MASSACHUSETTS, USA **TECHNIQUES** CAD SOFTWARE, METAL SINTERING **MATERIALS** SINTERED STEEL WITH BRONZE INFILTRATION, POLYAMIDE NYLON **WEBSITE** BATHSHEBA.COM

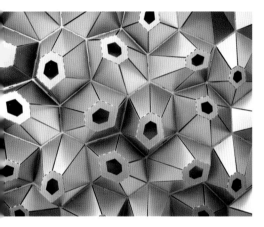

GT2P

BLENDING THE DIGITAL WORLD
AND INDIGENOUS CRAFT CULTURE

ABOVE
Shhh the Hope Keeper,
laser-cut sheets of gold
anodized aluminium

OPPOSITE
Royal Mahuida (top), die-cast
in bronze from 3D-printed
moulds; *Shhh the Hope Keeper*
(bottom)

The eclectic works produced by the designers of GT2P ('great things to people') are conceived through research and exploration into the concept of 'digital crafting', combining cutting-edge fabrication technologies with the craft traditions and cultural heritage of their native Chile.

The studio's metalworking output includes *Royal Mahuida* (opposite, top), created as a tribute to the ancient Inca people, who, according to legend, buried their gold in the forest. The designs were derived from the growth patterns of trees and sculpted in CAD, before moulds were 3D-printed and the final pieces die-cast in bronze. *Shhh the Hope Keeper* (left and opposite, bottom), a container for wishes and secrets, mimics a tessellating colony of crustaceans and was mathematically generated by computer, then laser-cut in sheet aluminium and shaped by hand.

Together with Guto Requena (p. 208) and Ariel Rojo (p. 214), the studio initiated the collaborative project *Losing My America* to build bridges between indigenous craft culture and the digitized commercial world. For the first exhibition, GT2P presented the work of Teresa Olmedo, whose family have been potters for five generations. The studio 3D-scanned an original clay figurine, manipulating the pixels to increase the digitized effect, before 3D-printing and hand-painting the result.

Ceramic work includes *Tarrugao* (overleaf), a collection of vases sculpted to capture the 'moment of a hug', impressed on a soft surface. Parametrically designed in CAD and then 3D-printed, the final pieces are then slip-cast in fine local porcelain.

LOCATION SANTIAGO, CHILE **TECHNIQUES** CAD-MODELLING, LASER-CUTTING, 3D-SCANNING, 3D-PRINTING, DIE-CASTING, SLIP-CASTING **MATERIALS** GOLD ANODIZED ALUMINIUM, BRONZE, POLYAMIDE NYLON, PORCELAIN **WEBSITE** GT2P.COM

'We realized that our work acquires a new value when we mix technology with traditional knowledge. Contrasting our digital expertise with the skills of craftsmanship has strengthened our output and enriched every design rule that we develop.'

THESE PAGES
Tarrugao, slip-cast in porcelain from 3D-printed moulds

MICHAEL HANSMEYER

CLASSICAL FORMS WITH THE POWER OF COMPUTATIONAL DESIGN

THESE PAGES
Sixth Order, 2011, a series
of elaborate architectural
columns

Architect Michael Hansmeyer, along with colleague Benjamin Dillenburger, is leading the way in the application of advanced digital-fabrication tools to the sculpting of complex architectural designs. For *Sixth Order* (these pages), made for the Gwangju Biennale 2011, in South Korea, Hansmeyer used computer algorithms and CNC laser-cutting to devise and construct a series of elaborate columns, drawing on classical orders, but with complex, manipulated geometries made possible through the digital technique of 'computational architecture'.

Each column in the series weighs about 900 kg (2,000 lbs), features a staggering eight million polygonal facets, modelled in CAD, and is constructed from 2,700 cross-sectional sheets of laser-cut ABS plastic. The central hole and outer contour of each cardboard slice were laser-cut, and the layers then stacked in order by sliding them onto vertical steel cores for stability. Hansmeyer is currently working on a load-bearing version in 3D-printed, stone threads.

For *Digital Grotesque Grotto* (overleaf), Hansmeyer fabricated his first full-scale 3D-printed room, a 20m² (215 sq ft) construction inspired by Gothic embellishment, and made possible through computational design. The digital model for the complex architectural form is a curious structure with no front or side elevations, which could not be fully realized, even on screen, owing to the 300 million individual facets involved. Once sliced into individual building blocks, the full data set was transferred to the printer, revealing the level of detail. The blocks, printed in a synthetic stone made from resin-bonded sand, were then stacked and the joints finished to present the final full-scale work.

LOCATION ZURICH, SWITZERLAND **TECHNIQUES** CAD-MODELLING, CNC LASER-CUTTING, 3D-PRINTING **MATERIALS** ABS PLASTIC, SYNTHETIC SANDSTONE **WEBSITE** MICHAEL-HANSMEYER.COM

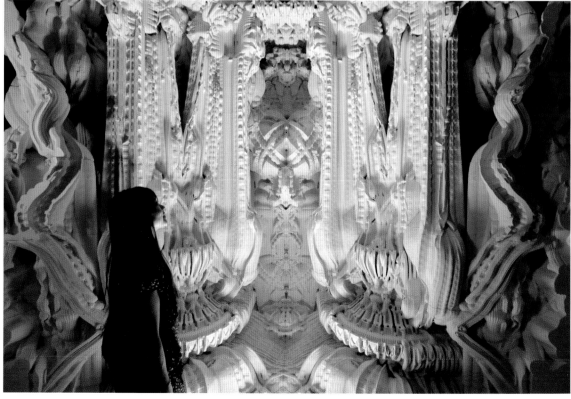

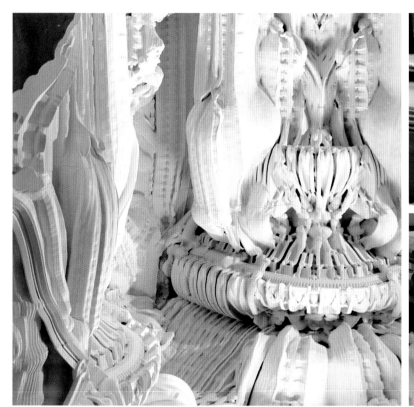

THESE PAGES
Digital Grotesque Grotto, 2013,
3D-printed in synthetic sandstone

'In architecture, digital-fabrication tools allow us to
bring back complex forms and systems of ornament
that previously were prohibitively expensive and
time-consuming. They let us work at the threshold
of haptic and visual perception.'

JOSHUA HARKER

THE INTRICACY OF HAND-SCULPTING WITH NEW MATERIAL TECHNOLOGIES

ABOVE
*Crania Anatomica Filigre:
Me to You*, 2011, 3D-printed to
order in polyamide nylon

OPPOSITE
Mazzo di Fiori, 2014,
limited-edition series,
3D-printed in polyamide nylon

Artist Joshua Harker, known for his 'pursuit of process', digitally sculpts his pioneering pieces with CAD software tools to shape the objects as he would a piece of clay or wood – he uses no computer-generated techniques or shortcuts. The resulting sculptures are then realized in coloured polyamide (nylon and glass powder), cast bronze and silver, and, more recently, gold-plated sintered steel, using a combination of both traditional and new fabrication techniques.

For *Tangle* (p. 101), Harker's landmark series of bronzes, a perfected exercise in the level of complexity only attainable with new fabrication technologies, each digital sculpture is first printed in PMMA (polymethyl methacrylate) powder using the additive layering technique. Because of the complexity of the sculptures, any broken models from the print process cannot be repaired and must be completely rebuilt. The final model is then utilized in the traditional lost-wax process of casting the final bronze sculpture, which is sandblasted and hand-polished.

In 2011, embracing a new era in the relationship between art and its audience, Harker's skull sculpture *Crania Anatomica Filigre: Me to You* was recorded as the Kickstarter crowd-funding website's most-funded sculpture project to date, raising 15,454 per cent of its target. This little piece marked Harker's first exploration of his now synonymous, surrealist style. It is made to order using selective laser-sintering in polyamide – with limited editions created in cast silver, gold-plated cast brass and gold-plated sintered steel.

LOCATION CHICAGO, ILLINOIS, USA **TECHNIQUES** CAD SOFTWARE,
LASER-SINTERING **MATERIALS** POLYAMIDE NYLON, CAST BRONZE,
SINTERED METALS **WEBSITE** JOSHHARKER.COM

'Over time, digital tools have become more intuitive in the way they have been developed for use by artists, rather than engineers. For me, they are simply a new set of tools for my art, and require just as much skill as traditional techniques of craftsmanship.'

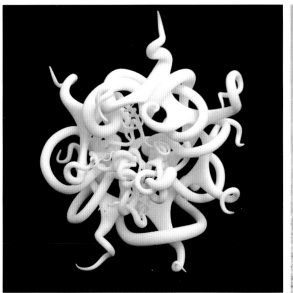

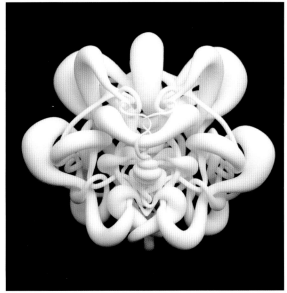

OPPOSITE
Crania Revolutis, 2012,
3D-printed to order in polyamide nylon

ABOVE
Delicated Ingress (top), 2011, and *Permutation Prime*
(bottom), 2013, from the *Tangle* series, made to order
in polyamide nylon and cast bronze

'The way that I think while writing computer code feels very different from the way I think while throwing a form on the potter's wheel. The pace of making affects the pace of thoughts, which affects the content. But all of these tools have their own intrinsic qualities.'

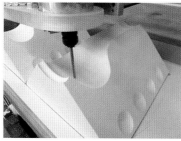

DEL HARROW

BREATHING LIFE INTO FINE PORCELAIN FORMS

Inspired by two different vessels in the collection of the Victoria & Albert Museum, London, and taking the element of air as his theme, artist Del Harrow created *Air_Breath* for the *Elemental* exhibition at the Northern Clay Center in Minneapolis, Minnesota. In creating his ceramic installation, Harrow explored the concept of 'pottery breathing'; 'breath' being a term often used by artisans when referring to the form and proportion of a pot.

He chose the V&A's two pots as a starting point, as each seemed to exemplify the process of breathing: one exhaled; one inhaled. Harrow then created a line of pots that captured a series of moments in the transition from one extreme of breathing to the other. First modelled as a CAD animation, which showed a virtual pot 'breathing', a 3D template file was then detailed for each of a series of frozen moments from the animation, creating the series of shapes.

The entire series of pots was then produced from a single plaster mould. Each vase was cast from a porcelain slip, into this mould, which was carved reductively using a CNC router. Starting by carving the block of plaster to cast the thinnest pot, after each cast the body of the plaster mould was gradually ground away to create more and more bulbous pot shapes.

ABOVE
Reductive carving of the plaster mould, using CNC-milling technology

LOCATION PENNSYLVANIA, USA **PROJECT** *AIR_BREATH* (2013)
TECHNIQUES CAD-MODELLING, CNC MILLING **MATERIALS** PLASTER, PORCELAIN **WEBSITE** DELHARROW.NET

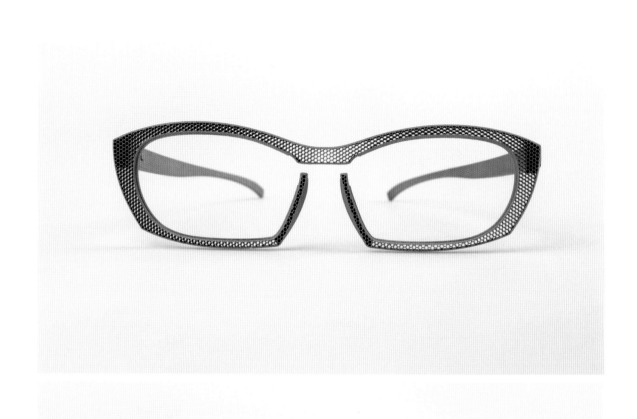

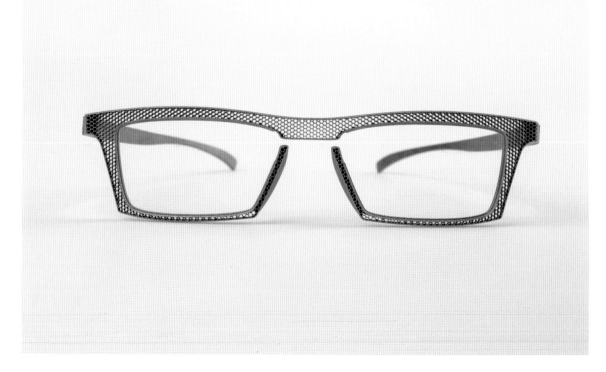

'It is obvious that digital technologies will gain importance versus hand skills in the creation of products. Craftsmanship is increasingly rarified, and thus more expensive, while the quality of digitally produced products is getting better and better. With time, digital craft will become a widely accepted mode of production.'

PATRICK HOET

COUTURE CRAFTSMANSHIP BREAKS NEW GROUND

After four years in development, the first couture glasses to be made using direct metal-sintering were launched in Belgium by the renowned designer and optician Patrick Hoet in 2014. The 'Made in Belgium' series is custom-printed in titanium, to the exact measurements of the customer, and was initially available in two models, *Homme I* and *Femme I*.

The front of the frames is formed from a fine honeycomb structure, which gives a semi-transparent appearance, while the ear pieces feature titanium shape-memory alloy springs. It would be nearly impossible to achieve a similar combination of aesthetic and quality using traditional frame-making techniques, and the concept also benefits from being eco-friendly: no stock needs to be produced and stored, and the only glasses fabricated are those that have been bought.

New designs are being introduced to the collection as the studio further challenges and refines their use of 3D-printing technologies.

LOCATION BRUGES, BELGIUM **TECHNIQUES** DIRECT METAL SINTERING, HAND-FINISHING **MATERIALS** TITANIUM **WEBSITE** HOET.EU

'Digital tools are a great aid, but a designer should also trust his hands. For me, digital tools speed up the process of making decisions, but the design itself (such as surfaces and proportions) must first be modelled by hand, to retain heart in a product, before being translated into a CAD model.'

RALF HOLLEIS

PRECISION ENGINEERING WITH A CRAFTSMAN'S TOUCH

THESE PAGES
VRZ 2, 2013, featuring bespoke 3D-printed lugs in laser-cused titanium, with a gold, black or silver ceramic coating

Combining advanced additive manufacturing with classic frame-building techniques, Ralf Holleis is the designer behind the VORWaeRTZ brand of bespoke carbon-fibre track bikes, which feature statement titanium fixtures crafted to meet the exact requirements of each rider. The lugs, fork crowns, hubs, brake bridges and seat-post parts are individually designed in CAD, allowing the fixings of each to be precisely angled to fit the specific dimensions and geometry of each bespoke frame.

Each piece is then fabricated in laser-cused titanium, which gives a material density of 99.8 per cent, much stronger than a conventional die-cast piece. This process speeds up the production time usually required for custom-made bike frames considerably. The computer-optimized lattice design also reduces the weight of the parts while maintaining structural strength.

The final lugs are sanded, polished and finished with a tough gold TiN (Titanium nitride), black TiCN (Titanium Carbo-nitride) or silver CrN (Chromium nitride) ceramic coating, before being fitted and bonded to the custom-cut carbon-frame elements. The fixings support the carbon tube inside and out – a complex design that could not be produced without digital tools. For the finishing touch, the whole bike is hand-finished with a transparent ceramic coating and fitted with a handmade carbon saddle.

LOCATION BISCHOFSGRÜN, GERMANY **TECHNIQUES** CAD-MODELLING, LASER CUSING, HAND-FINISHING **MATERIALS** TITANIUM, CARBON FIBRE, CERAMIC COATINGS **WEBSITE** VORWAERTZ.COM

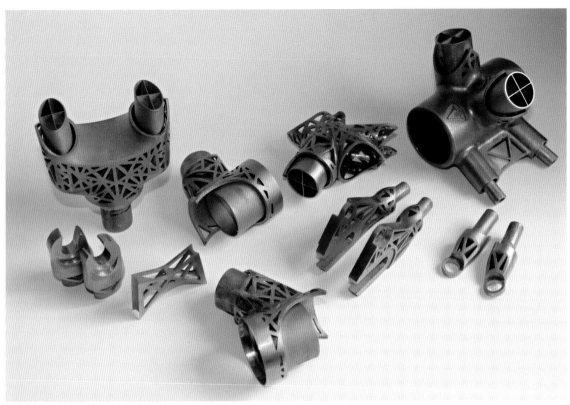

ABOVE
Finished titanium lugs, complete with gold ceramic coating, before assembly

LEFT
Laser-cused titanium lugs, still with integrated support structure from the print process, before sanding and polishing

'Without digital technology I would never have created my current artworks. I simply could not have calculated the multiplication and precise blending in a traditional setting. It is so important to work across fields, so you place no restriction on the final artwork.'

MONIKA HORCICOVÁ

THE COLLISION OF BODY, SCIENCE AND ART

Artist Monika Horcicová explores themes of infinity and our relationship to our skeletal structure as a thing of beauty, rather than morbidity – an exploration that has culminated in a growing collection of scale model works, suggesting a technologically advanced ossuary. She utilizes digital technologies as an integral part of the conception process to minimize the restrictions around developing and modelling each complex arrangement.

The scale models are conceived using highly detailed, computer-generated bone structures, which Horcicová manipulates and fuses together into the final skeletal formations. These formations are then printed in polyamide nylon and sanded, before being used to create silicone moulds from which the final resin sculptures are cast.

While some of the simpler works are cast as a single entity, others require a more complicated process of calculation and construction. For Horcicová's BA thesis project *Wheel of Life* (opposite, top), each leg was printed and cast separately; the position and angles of each joint individually calculated and taken from the complete digital model. They were then assembled into the final formation by hand, with each leg attached to a central circular core, produced as a single piece.

For *Pelvis* (opposite, bottom right), each part was again calculated and cast individually, before being slotted together like a three-dimensional jigsaw puzzle to create the final form.

OPPOSITE
Wheel of Life (top), 2012, and *Pelvis* (bottom right), 2013, cast in polyurethane resin from 3D-printed moulds

LOCATION BRNO, CZECH REPUBLIC **TECHNIQUES** CAD-MODELLING, SELECTIVE LASER-SINTERING, TRADITIONAL CASTING **MATERIALS** POLYURETHANE RESIN, PLASTER COMPOSITE **WEBSITE** MONIKAHORCICOVA.WORDPRESS.COM

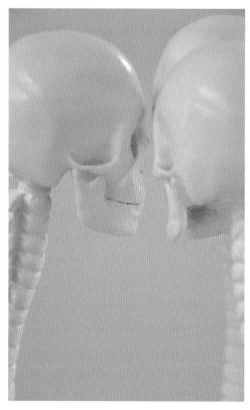 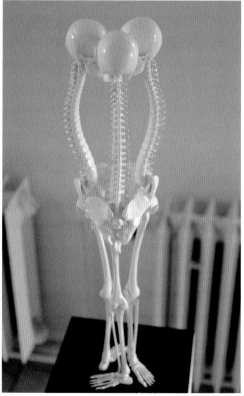

ABOVE
Communication Cycle, 2011, plaster composite

OPPOSITE
Leg and Hand, 2013, and *Chests* (top), 2013,
cast in polyurethane resin from 3D-printed
moulds; *Communication Cycle* (bottom)

'My practice as a ceramicist integrates technology and tradition. Though I make work that involves industrial techniques and new technologies, each end product is labour-intensive and unique.'

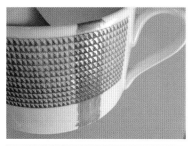

ANTHONY HORRIGAN

TECHNOLOGICAL EMBELLISHMENT OF A TRADITIONAL CRAFT

The work of ceramicist Anthony Horrigan explores the creative potential of laser-etching directly onto the glazed surface of bone china. The engraved surface is then gilded in precious metals.

The first project made using this process, *Amalgam*, is a collection of lidded canisters, stemmed bowls and vases, inspired by Japanese bark tea caddies, as well as by prehistoric Celtic metalwork and the traditional acid etching process – a beautiful technique rarely used today, owing to its irregular results and the potentially hazardous effects of the production process.

The plain shapes are cast in fine bone china in Staffordshire, home to this traditional material for over two hundred years. After firing, the glazed surfaces are decorated with intricate geometric patterns of laser-engraved lines, with each canister held horizontally and rotated while the laser 'draws' lines across the curved surface. Once engraved, the vessels are gilded in 24-carat gold or platinum, bringing out the texture of the etching.

Initially researched as part of his MA studies, Horrigan's unique technique in creating the *Amalgam* collection went on to win the Future Makers Innovation Award from the Crafts Council of Ireland.

LOCATION STOKE-ON-TRENT, UK **TECHNIQUES** TRADITIONAL CHINA CASTING, LASER-ETCHING, GILDING **MATERIALS** BONE CHINA, GOLD AND PLATINUM GILDING **WEBSITE** CARGOCOLLECTIVE.COM/ANTHONYHORRIGAN

'For me, 3D tools provide an immediate response to my ideas – they can play back different forms as fast as my thinking can develop them. It allows me to challenge the possibilities of complicated forms that are beyond the ability of the brain and eye to conceive.'

DORRY HSU

INDUSTRIAL TECHNOLOGY MEETS THE IMAGINED WORLD

BELOW
Aesthetic of Fears, 2013

OPPOSITE
A selection of works from the *Aesthetic of Fears* collection (top and middle rows); *Future Jewelry* (bottom row)

Inspired by her fear of insects, artist and accessories designer Dorry Hsu created the *Aesthetic of Fears* collection as a modern interpretation of the cultural tradition of wearing masks to ward off evil. Alongside many-legged bugs, the symmetrical forms and graduated colours of the pieces draw inspiration from crystalline structures and the symmetry of Rorschach prints.

Each curious insect-like form is first conceived using modelling software linked to a haptic arm, a tool that allows Hsu to sculpt the virtual objects on screen just as she would a lump of clay. When moving the arm, which functions like a computer mouse, the user can feel the dragging tension of the virtual clay.

The digital models are then prepared for print and transferred to a stereolithographic printer, to be sculpted in plain, clear resin. The pixel marks from the process are deliberately left on the surface of the finished object, rather than being polished out, to add another level of texture. Each piece is then coloured by hand using a unique, time-intensive method of dipping into boiling dye – adding one hue at a time to build up the final colour gradients, which enhance the dimensions of each piece. This colouring process takes an average of three hours.

Once cooled, the pieces are finished with the addition of latex straps. Another benefit of digital modelling is that the pieces can be fitted to the wearer's shape before being made, ensuring a comfortable fit upon completion, with no further shaping required.

LOCATION LONDON, UK **TECHNIQUES** 3D-MODELLING SOFTWARE WITH HAPTIC ARM, 3D-PRINTING, HAND DIP-DYEING **MATERIALS** RESIN, COLOURED DYES **WEBSITE** DORRYHSU.COM

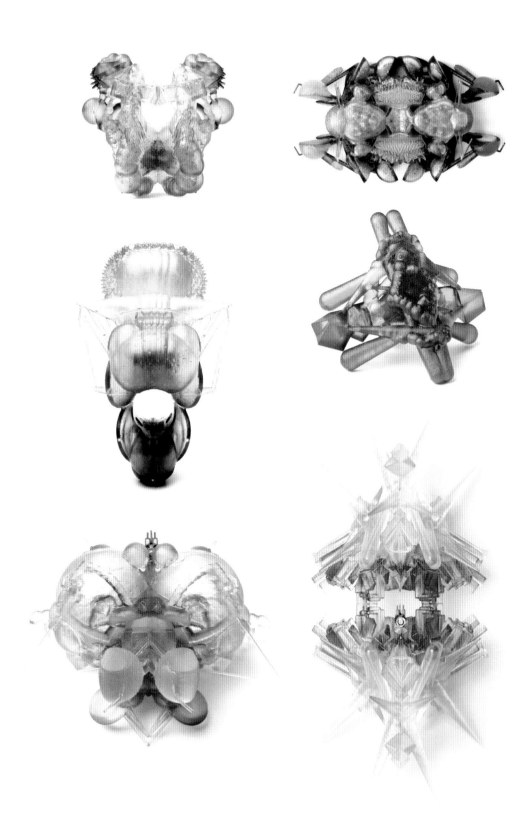

INFLEXIONS

MIXING THE EFFECTS OF TRADITIONAL AND DIGITAL KNOWLEDGE

OPPOSITE
Eclipse (top), 2014, with
touch-sensitive ceramic panel,
coated with a conductive glaze;
the central panel (bottom),
CNC-milled in porcelain, then
glazed and fired

As part of a three-month residency at the New Taipei City Yingge Ceramics Museum for the Taiwan Ceramics Biennale, French design duo Inflexions explored the impact of digital-fabrication technologies on the production of ceramics. Expanding on their approach of customizing existing digital tools to effect new outputs, the pair trialled new systems for the conception of ceramic objects, in which customers control the creative output.

For the *Cutting Edge* plate collection (overleaf), users interact with the process by using a multi-touch application on a tablet computer to choose the desired sizes and number of plates. The plates are then translated into three-dimensional form using CNC-milling technology to cut out and carve each one from a standard slip-cast porcelain blank, which is then glazed and fired. These blanks are cast from a specially designed plaster mould, cut by the CNC machine.

For another project, *Back to Back* (overleaf), the designers used a Kinect infrared camera to track and record hand gestures (for example, mimicking the potter's wheel), which are then interpreted as a pattern on the surface of the final piece. These patterns are CNC-milled onto the surfaces of bisque porcelain platters, and glazed and fired.

Taking their fascination with mixing tradition and technology further, the *Eclipse* wall lamp (opposite) features a tactile central disc, again CNC-milled in Japanese porcelain clay and coated with a conductive glaze. After firing, this glazed panel acts as a sensor for touch; the user gently runs his or her fingers around the rim of the disc to slowly adust the brightness of the light.

LOCATION BAGNOLET, FRANCE **TECHNIQUES** CNC-MILLING, GLAZING, FIRING **MATERIALS** JAPANESE PORCELAIN **WEBSITE** IN-FLEXIONS.COM

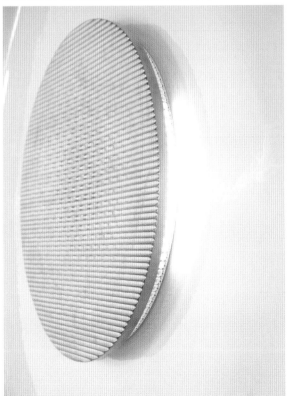

TOP AND BOTTOM

Cutting Edge, 2014. The collection allows the customer to interact with the manufacturing process and choose the size of each plate before it is made

ABOVE

Back to Back, 2014. For this collection of plates, the designers used a Kinect infrared camera to capture the motions of the potter's wheel

'Our work is not only about fabricating pieces using digital tools, but also about imagining new ways of conceiving those pieces through digital interactions. We choose our tools for the best outcome, meeting somewhere between traditional and digital knowledge.'

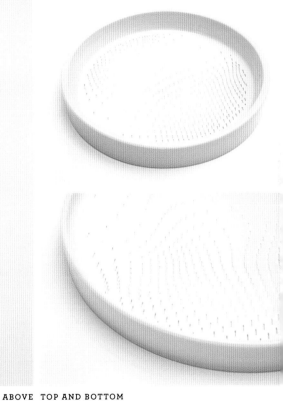

ABOVE
The design of the *Back to Back* collection has customizable patterning, made using CNC-milling technology

TOP AND BOTTOM
The *Cutting Edge* collection of stacking plates is made to order in specified sizes

'3D-scanning and 3D-printing enable me to make objects that I could never have made so well by hand, and bring to life things I could previously only imagine. They have given me a new relationship with my work.'

AKI INOMATA

THE NATURAL WORLD MEETS HUMAN CIVILIZATION IN MINIATURE FORM

For *Why Not Hand Over a Shelter to Hermit Crabs?*, artist Aki Inomata created tiny cityscapes as temporary accommodation for hermit crabs, which move from one shell to another as they outgrow each one. Keeping the welfare of the crabs central to the project, natural sea shells were used as the basis of each piece. The shells were CT-scanned to create a digital model of the interior spiral, ensuring the volume of the space was suitable as a home.

Around this central space, Inomata digitally modelled a series of miniature urbanscapes, each integrated into the shell's exterior surface – representing the skyline of New York, Dutch windmills and Bangkok temples, among others. The shells were then produced in non-toxic, clear resin, formed and cured using the process of stereolithography. Each transparent shell – allowing the crab's body to be partially visible through the material – was then cleaned and polished before being placed into a terrarium tank, where the crabs were left to discover and choose for themselves an embellished shell of their liking.

The resulting temporary pairings of crab and shell were photographed for a gallery presentation. The crabs later discarded their resin shells in favour of larger ones, as they continued their evolution.

LOCATION TOKYO, JAPAN **TECHNIQUES** CT-SCANNING, CAD-MODELLING, STEREOLITHOGRAPHY, HAND-FINISHING **MATERIALS** RESIN **WEBSITE** AKI-INOMATA.COM

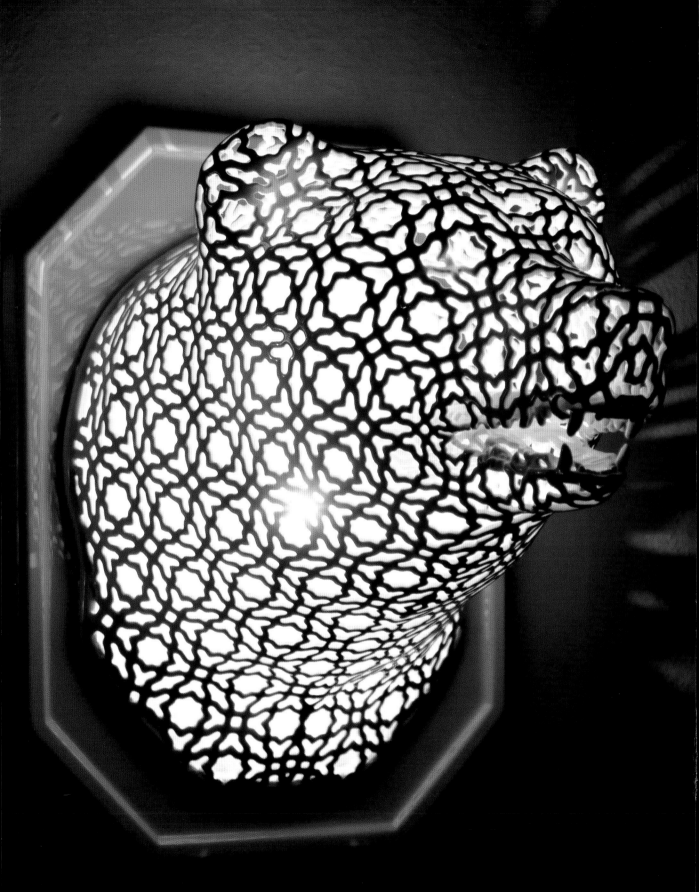

LINLIN & PIERRE-YVES JACQUES

THE DIGITAL EMBELLISHMENT OF NATURAL BEAUTY

ABOVE
Bird Travel, limited edition, 3D-printed in polyamide nylon

OPPOSITE
Bear, part of the limited-edition *Animal-lace* collection, 3D-printed in polyamide nylon

Combining qualifications in digital design and 3D video production, respectively, and bringing 'four hands and two heads' to every project, Linlin and Pierre-Yves Jacques create fantastical lighting designs and sculptural curiosities, which are a tribute to both the beauty of nature and the potential of refined digital manufacture. To do so, the pair cross cultures and historical references, and bring their fascination with Asian artistry to each project.

The recognizable animal forms from the *Animal-lace* series (opposite and p. 126), are carved first as digital sculptures, which have been worked in minute detail to create the impression of moulded lacework. The resulting designs are then brought to life in polyamide nylon using selective laser-sintering. Each sculpture is made individually, as a single piece, to order.

The pair's latest project, *Goldfishes* (p. 127), challenges expectations of the quality of 3D-printed objects. They explore options for the highest-quality finishing of the artwork after fabrication, thereby promising a closer translation from idea to reality. In this case, the digital sculpture has been printed and cured in photopolymer resin, using the high-definition stereolithography technique, before the final design is painted in Klein Blue, gilded in 24-carat gold and polished.

LOCATION PARIS, FRANCE **TECHNIQUES** CAD-MODELLING, LASER-SINTERING, STEREOLITHOGRAPHY, HAND-FINISHING **MATERIALS** POLYAMIDE NYLON, PHOTOPOLYMER RESIN, 24-CARAT GOLD **WEBSITE** LPJACQUES.COM

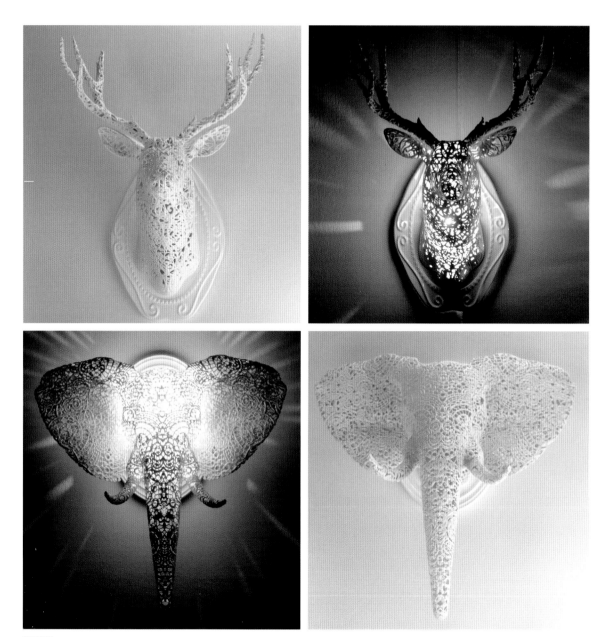

ABOVE
Deer (top) and *Elephant* (bottom), from the limited-edition
Animal-lace collection, 3D-printed in polyamide nylon

OPPOSITE
Goldfishes, limited-edition triptych, 3D-printed in resin,
painted and 24-carat gold-plated

'How do you view digital tools,
versus handcraft skills perhaps,
and their impact on your
sculptural work?'

127

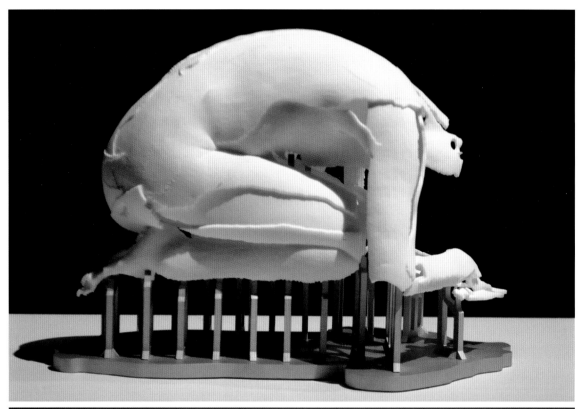

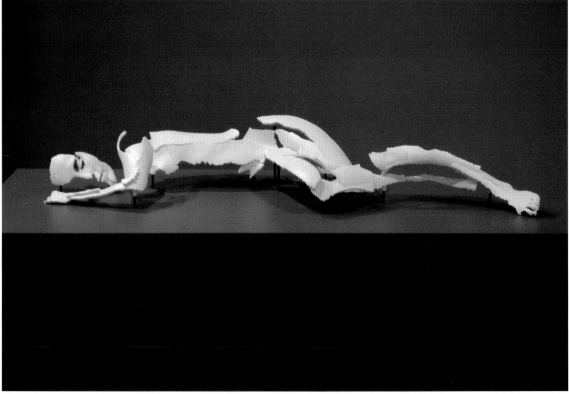

'I am interested in using technology critically, working at the limits of what it was designed to do. Every artistic material and medium resists our attempts to perfect it, leaving the marks of the maker. I try to find those marks in digital media.'

SOPHIE KAHN

SEEKING THE PERFECT IMPERFECTIONS OF A CONTEMPORARY MAKER'S TOOLS

OPPOSITE
Période de Délire, K (top), 2014, 30 × 28 × 20 cm (12 × 11 × 8 in.); *Reclining Figure of a Woman (Five Years of Sleep)* (bottom), 2013, life size, 3D-prints from 3D laser-scans

Artist Sophie Kahn has been exploring the possibilities of 3D-scanning and 3D-printing for more than ten years. Where many artists look to contrast technology with historical art influences, her explorations of the nude female body – and heightened emotional content, such as madness, illness and death – present a powerful contrast with the detached processes of contemporary fabrication.

Each sculpture begins with the creation of a digital model, using a hand-held 3D laser-scanner to capture the model's pose. Kahn deliberately misuses this precisely engineered device, resulting in fragmented, incomplete scans that capture the motion blur of a body in constant flux. The image files are then edited, rearranged, layered and prepared for printing, a painstaking process that involves assembling and repairing the tiniest digital details, which can take several weeks.

Once the digital model is complete, each seemingly fragile construction of fragments is 3D-printed in polyamide, ceramic plaster or sintered metal, often as one piece. Each sculpture is then hand-finished, by sanding or painting, before being assembled on a metal framework to present the final work. For some sculptures, Kahn will make a silicone mould around the original 3D-printed form, from which she creates a wax cast. This is used to create a cast in bronze, using the lost-wax method.

LOCATION NEW YORK, NEW YORK, USA **TECHNIQUES** LASER-SCANNING, CAD-MODELLING, LASER-SINTERING, WAX AND BRONZE CASTING **MATERIALS** POLYAMIDE NYLON, CERAMIC, BRONZE **WEBSITE** SOPHIEKAHN.NET

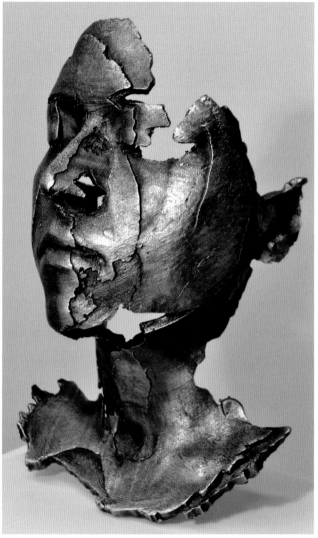

ABOVE
L:Degrade (top left), 2012, life size; *L:Gold (right)*, 2012,
life size, bronze casts from 3D prints

OPPOSITE
Bust of a Woman, Head Thrown Back, 2013, life size,
3D print from 3D laser-scan

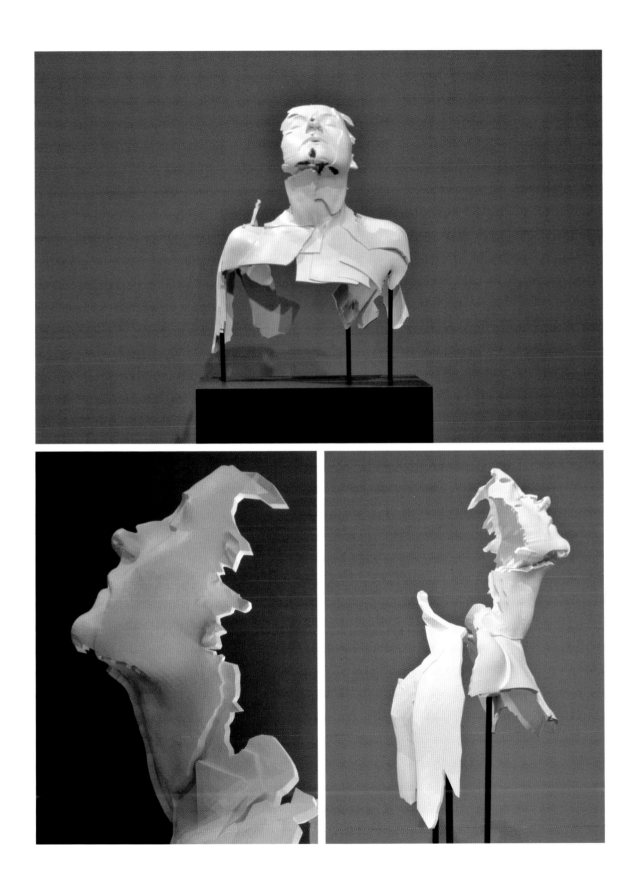

JORIS
LAARMAN

OPPOSITE, TOP LEFT
Aluminium Gradient, 2014,
from the *Microstructures* series

**OPPOSITE, TOP RIGHT
AND BOTTOM**
Makerchair series, 2014, made
from digitally fabricated pieces
that can be downloaded from
bitsandparts.org

Furniture designer Joris Laarman is a true pioneer in the exploration
of digital-fabrication technologies – not just as a tool for industrial
prototyping or creative exploration, but also for manufacturing
high-quality, consumer-ready products, on an individual basis.

The *Microstructures* series – including the *Aluminium Gradient*
(opposite, top left) and *Soft Gradient* chairs, the first to be 3D-printed
in polyurethane foam and aluminium, respectively – is a response to the
increasing ubiquity of 3D-printing by challenging the material quality of
the resulting forms. The designs demand subtle detailing in the material
structure created during the printing process, through tiny building
blocks that are graduated in size, porosity, thickness, flexibility and
rigidity, resulting in sculpted, tactile and flexible surfaces.

Responding to the emerging potential of consumer-ready designs,
which can be made by the end users themselves, the *Makerchair* series
of chairs (opposite and p. 134) are designed to be built from small,
digitally fabricated three-dimensional parts that fit together like a jigsaw
puzzle. By fractioning the designs into many small components, Laarman
has radically expanded the potential of small consumer 3D-printers and
CNC-milling machines to create large-format but lightweight bespoke
objects in a multitude of materials and colours.

Reflecting Laarman's view that the *Makerchair* concept is a work
in progress, the blueprints of many of the designs are available on the
Internet, under a Creative Commons license, for anyone to download,
modify and make themselves.

LOCATION AMSTERDAM, NETHERLANDS **TECHNIQUES** CAD-MODELLING,
3D-PRINTING, CNC-MILLING **MATERIALS** POLYURETHANE FOAM, ALUMINIUM,
RESIN, MAPLE WOOD **WEBSITE** JORISLAARMAN.COM / BITSANDPARTS.ORG

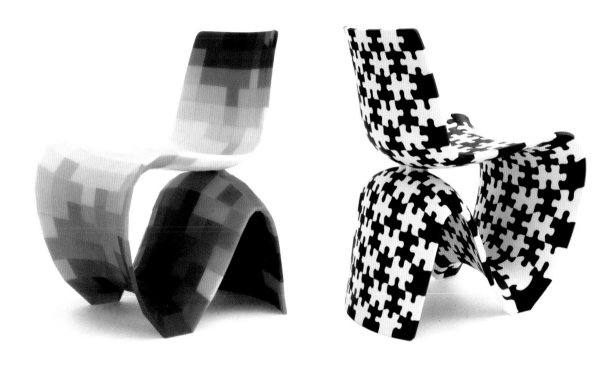

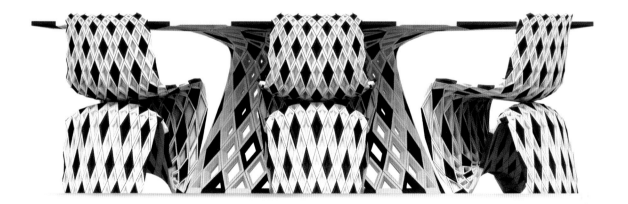

ABOVE
A table from the *Maker* furniture series, CNC-milled in small
pieces of wood, before being hand-assembled

OPPOSITE
The tiny jigsaw parts of the various *Makerchairs* designs,
3D-printed in ABS plastic (top left) or carved from wood
using CNC machines (top right)

'We believe in the symbiosis of handcraft and
technology. But regardless of how interesting the
development in digital fabrication technologies might
be, we feel it is still in its infancy. Digital fabrication
needs to scale up in order to grow up.'

CINNAMON LEE

THE SPLICING OF ROMANCE
AND ENGINEERING

ABOVE
Covert Romantic, 2014,
from the *Tough Love* collection
of laser-sintered titanium rings

OPPOSITE
Clockwise from top left:
Blue Flowers, 2009, *Secret
Love*, 2010, and *Hidden
Squareness*, 2008, all from the
Secrets series; *Hexar*, 2010, and
Quadross, 2010

Exploring the evolving relationship between hand and machine, artist Cinnamon Lee's approach to jewelry design combines digital-manufacturing processes with traditional, highly accomplished metalsmithing techniques. She has been working with precious metals for over fifteen years, experimenting with digital-manufacturing tools, and her work has been acquired by many public collections, including the National Gallery of Australia.

Lee's work took a pioneering path when she discovered the technology for high-resolution plotted wax printing, which enables the crafting of precise, highly detailed structures. Combining this revolutionizing process with the conventional lost-wax method of casting has led to her trademark 'hidden' designs, in which the textured pattern on the exterior surface of a ring transforms into a different pattern on the interior – an effect that would be impossible to achieve using traditional fabrication techniques. The resulting wax models are then cast in silver and hand-polished, with the detail picked out in coloured enamels.

Lee continues to investigate the impact of digital-fabrication processes on the traditions of jewelry design. Recently, she has employed selective laser-sintering technology to create incredibly fine designs in titanium, in one piece and without the need for a mould, including the *Tough Love* collection, which features the *Superstructure* ring (p. 139), and the *Super Solitaire* series.

LOCATION SYDNEY, AUSTRALIA **TECHNIQUES** CAD SOFTWARE, PLOTTED WAX PRINTING, LASER-SINTERING, WAX CASTING, ENAMELLING **MATERIALS** SILVER, TITANIUM, ENAMELS **WEBSITE** CINNAMONLEE.COM

ABOVE
Covert Jewels series, 2011, in 925 silver, oxidized,
highlighted with coloured display lighting

OPPOSITE
The seemingly fragile *Superstructure* ring, 2014,
3D-printed in laser-sintered titanium

'I pick out ideas that are a product of the process being used – which could not be produced using conventional means and, perhaps more importantly, would not have been conceived with conventional knowledge.'

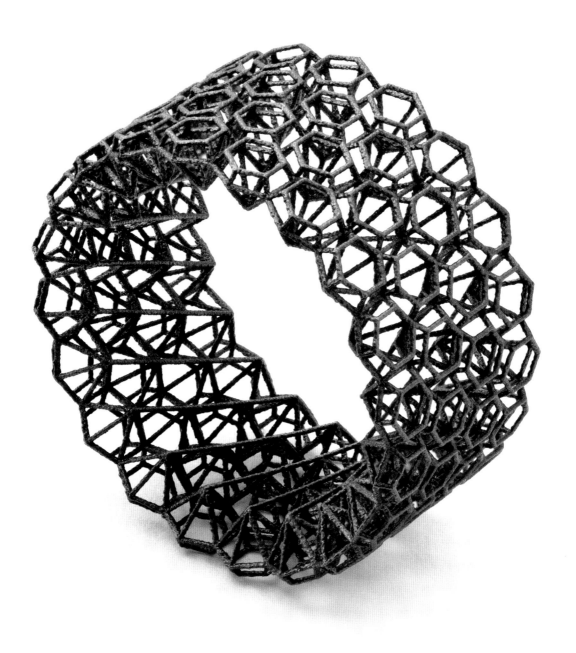

LEE ALLEN EYEWEAR

BRINGING A NEW ETIQUETTE TO AN ARTISANAL INDUSTRY

Lee Allen Eyewear produces sophisticated, limited-edition eyewear, as well as bespoke pieces, using a combination of traditional machine technologies, cutting-edge digital tools and many steps of hand-finishing. Each frame is designed in CAD with a series of prototypes made up in thin chipboard using a laser-cutter, to adjust and confirm the optimum profile proportions across the fronts and temples of each piece.

The final designs for the frame fronts are then individually cut with a bespoke, refined CNC-router to ensure a perfectly symmetrical frame outline. The nose pads are laminated on, shaved down using a vintage French pad trimming machine, and filed by hand, before the frame front is placed in a tumbling unit for a period of six or seven days. Each frame front is then taken through a complex, time-intensive process of hand-finishing, which includes a combination of filing and polishing, depending on the material, to bring out a unique, mirror-like lustre in the material.

The temples of each frame are put through a similar production process, with a wire inserted into the acetate for adjustability and reinforcement, before the pieces are again shaped, tumbled and hand-polished. The frames are then ready for the final operation of marking, mitring and hand-assembly. The studio has also begun working with 3D-printing technologies, including laser-sintering in titanium, creating bespoke glasses designs with the same high attention to detail in the finishing.

ABOVE
Select designs from the CNC-routed and hand-finished range of vintage acetate frames

OPPOSITE, TOP
A CNC-routed, hand-finished frame design in vintage acetate

OPPOSITE, MIDDLE AND BOTTOM
Luce frame (2014), printed in laser-sintered titanium, and made specially for this book

LOCATION PROVIDENCE, RHODE ISLAND, AND BROOKLYN, NEW YORK, USA **TECHNIQUES** CAD-MODELLING, LASER-CUTTING, CNC-ROUTING, HAND-FINISHING **MATERIALS** VINTAGE ACETATE **WEBSITE** LEEALLENEYEWEAR.COM

'Today's creative tools provide us with a means of exploration that was only ever previously attainable by our collective imaginations. It is our belief, however, that a product remains incomplete until it has been touched by the human hand.'

'I see my work as the process of giving human meaning to material objects. My design method is a recombining of old and new ideas, so in this way I'm interested in applying innovative production processes to natural materials, for the purpose of humanizing new technology.'

PAUL LOEBACH

HUMANIZING TECHNOLOGY THROUGH THE MEDIUM OF WOOD

OPPOSITE
Vase Space (top), 2008, multi-axis CNC-machined in hard maple; *Chair-O-Space* (bottom), 2009, CNC-carved in hard maple

Descended from a long line of furniture makers, Paul Loebach creates furniture and objects that are infused with character and inventiveness, the result of contrasting traditional carpentry practice and decorative detailing with state-of-the-art digital milling technologies more usually used by the advanced engineering industries.

Loebach's classically inspired *Vase Space* table (opposite, top) integrates three removable wooden vases that flow into the grain of the tabletop, and was the result of a four-month collaboration with a US aerospace manufacturer, using multi-axis CNC-machining to create a single form from hard maple wood. In a similar collaboration, *Chair-O-Space* (opposite, bottom) and *Shelf Space* (p. 144) see traditional materials become apparently malleable, as the structures push the limits of wood engineering and advanced machining technology to create highly refined forms from blocks of hard maple and basswood.

For the *Wood Vases* series (p. 144), another experiment in CNC-machining, smaller blocks of maple are milled in two symmetrical halves and joined together with a feature 'parting line'. And responding to the challenge of shipping furniture as compactly and efficiently as possible, as well as drawing on the aesthetic of childhood toys, the chair design *PEG* (p. 145) embodies its acronym of 'parts excluding glue': it is CNC-milled in birch in eight precisely honed components, which are simply tapped into place in the final assembly.

LOCATION NEW YORK, USA, AND BERLIN, GERMANY **TECHNIQUES** CNC-MILLING, TRADITIONAL WOODWORKING AND FINISHING **MATERIALS** MAPLE, BASSWOOD, BIRCH **WEBSITE** PAULLOEBACH.COM

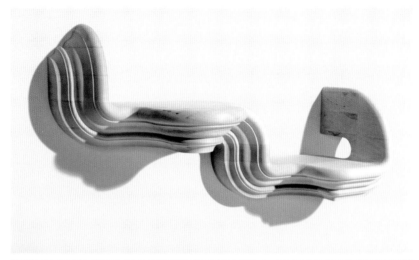

ABOVE
Shelf Space (top), 2008, CNC-carved in hard maple;
Wood Vases (bottom), 2009, CNC-milled in two
halves in hard maple

OPPOSITE
PEG, 2014, birch, easy-to-assemble chair

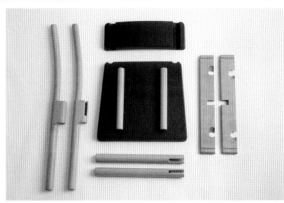

'I am intrigued by the way the introduction of digital techniques alters my work and informs the design process. Yet I value my freedom to combine new and traditional techniques. It forges a uniquely personal connection between the maker and the object.'

AMY ROPER LYONS

REIMAGINING A RARE ART OF MASTER CRAFTSMEN

ABOVE
Detail of the plique-à-jour enamelling technique

Jeweller and enamellist Amy Roper Lyons has been crafting one-of-a-kind decorative pieces for over twenty-five years. Originally focused on exploring traditional techniques with gold, silver, gemstones and enamels (for which she won the Grand Prize at the prestigious Saul Bell jewelry-design competition), her current body of work – a collection of enamelled vessels – uses digital technologies to aid the fabrication of the fine structures of her pieces.

Lyons designs and draws the structural forms of her decorative vessels to scale using 3D-modelling software, before 3D-printing the results in resin. From these prints, rubber moulds are taken before the final piece is cast in sterling silver. The more complicated and larger structures are printed and cast in sections, which are then welded together to achieve the final form. Each finished object is enamelled by hand, using the historic plique-à-jour technique. The first layer of enamel is fired, followed by a brief sintering in the kiln for each subsequent layer.

Meaning 'letting in light', plique-à-jour involves suspending vitreous enamels within the individual cells of a metal framework to create a richly coloured, translucent surface. Seen in the work of Fabergé, Lalique and other master craftsmen of the nineteenth and early twentieth centuries, this painstaking technique is rarely used today.

LOCATION NEW JERSEY, USA **TECHNIQUES** CAD-MODELLING, 3D-PRINTING, METAL CASTING, PLIQUE-À-JOUR **WEBSITE** AMYROPERLYONS.COM

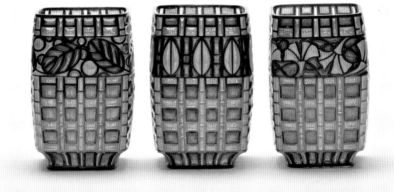

ABOVE
Luxor Bowl (top), 2013, plique-à-jour enamelling on sterling-silver structure, cast from a 3D-printed mould

OPPOSITE
A collection of goblets and vessels, plique-à-jour enamelling on sterling-silver structures, cast from 3D-printed moulds

'For me, it is not really relevant if a tool is digital or analogue, as long as it works for the end result I want to create. It is about making something that has not been done before. Tools rule!'

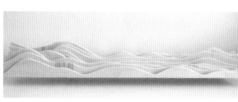

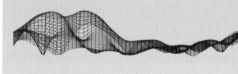

THESE PAGES
Brainwave Sofa, 2009,
CNC-milled foam

Designer Lucas Maassen's one-off creation, *Brainwave Sofa* (these pages), a collaboration with Dries Verbruggen (see p. 234), is created from an original electro-encephalogram (EEG) scan of his own Alpha brain waves, the rhythm of which is influenced by opening and closing the eyes.

The resulting waves were captured as a 3D landscaped image on screen, in which the depth of the wave is the frequency of brain-activity in Hertz (cycles per second), the height is the strength of the signal and the length marks the progression of time.

This three-dimensional data image was converted into a digital model, and sent to a CNC-milling machine that carved out the peaks and troughs of this 'brain landscape' in soft foam. Once complete, the shape was upholstered by hand in thick, warm grey felt with buttoned facings, and framed with pine.

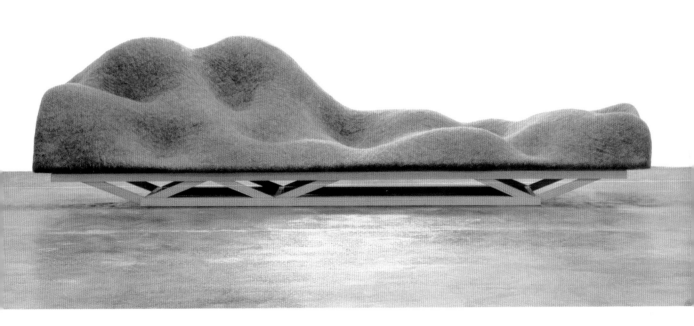

LUCAS
MAASSEN

CAPTURING THE INVISIBLE
IN TACTILE FORM

LOCATION EINDHOVEN, NETHERLANDS **PROJECT** *BRAINWAVE SOFA* (2009) **DIMENSIONS** 254 × 67 × 60 CM (100 × 26 × 24 IN.) **TECHNIQUES** CAD-MODELLING, EEG BRAIN-SCANNING, CNC-MILLING, UPHOLSTERY **MATERIALS** FOAM, FELT, PINE **WEBSITE** LUCASMAASSEN.NL

'When an artist like Chuck Close approaches the studio, I don't ask him about pixels and megabytes. He brings a concept and imagery, and I put every mark-making tool at his disposal. We are committed to exceptional art-making, and we believe that the tools of innovation and tradition are equally fundamental.'

MAGNOLIA EDITIONS

UNIQUE INNOVATION BROUGHT TO A TIME-HONOURED MEDIUM

ABOVE
Chuck Close, *Kate*, 2007
seen in production

OPPOSITE
Chuck Close, *Lou*, 2012,
236 × 198 cm (93 × 78 in.),
Jacquard tapestry in archival
cottons and viscose

Magnolia Editions, founded by artist and inventor Donald Farnsworth in 1981, works closely with world-renowned artists to enable their ideas across a variety of media and innovative production processes, from etching to digital printing and Jacquard weaving.

The tapestries created with artist Chuck Close (these pages and overleaf) begin as original photographs, which are scanned and converted into high-resolution digital files. These are then manipulated, before being translated into weave files. Farnsworth uses a 2.1 m (7 ft)-wide, double-headed Jacquard loom, which offers twice as many warp threads, and twice the density and maximum number of possible weave structures and colours. He and Close worked with a palette of up to five hundred colours per tapestry (less for black and white), selected from a sample palette of over two thousand possible weave structures. Adjustments were made throughout the weaving process, using the original palette as a guide.

Traditionally, the paint-by-numbers approach of mechanical weaving – mapping each coloured thread as a pixel in the weave file – resulted in an obvious woven texture across the surface of the tapestry. But Farnsworth wanted to create a new, highly refined aesthetic, so he adapted the method to allow the artist to create minutely detailed changes to the visuals onscreen, analysing the full image inch by inch, which the computer automatically translates into the corresponding program of binary code for the loom. The result is a woven image of very fine quality.

LOCATION OAKLAND, CALIFORNIA, USA **TECHNIQUES** DIGITAL JACQUARD WEAVING **MATERIALS** ARCHIVAL COTTONS, VISCOSE **WEBSITE** MAGNOLIAEDITIONS.COM

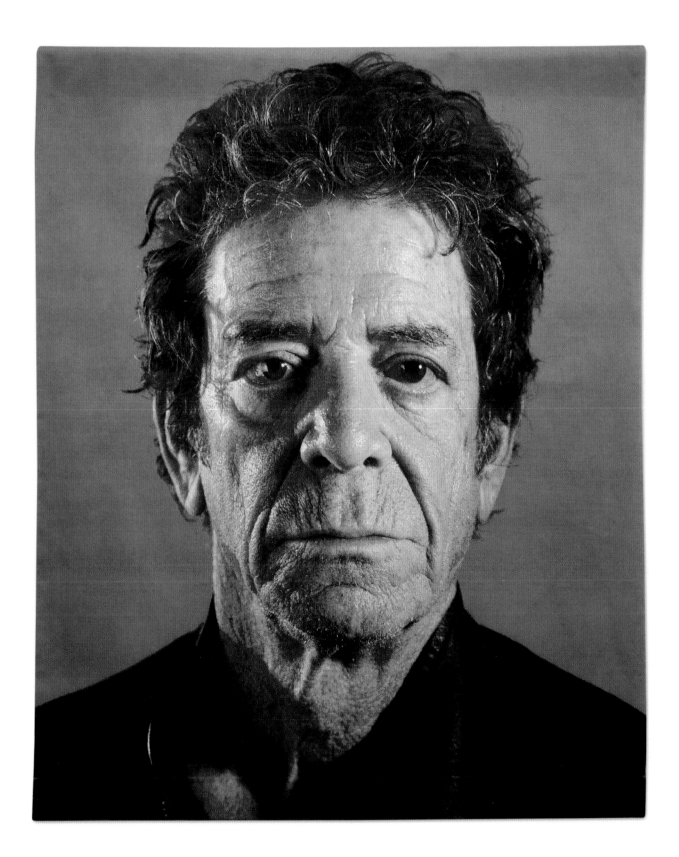

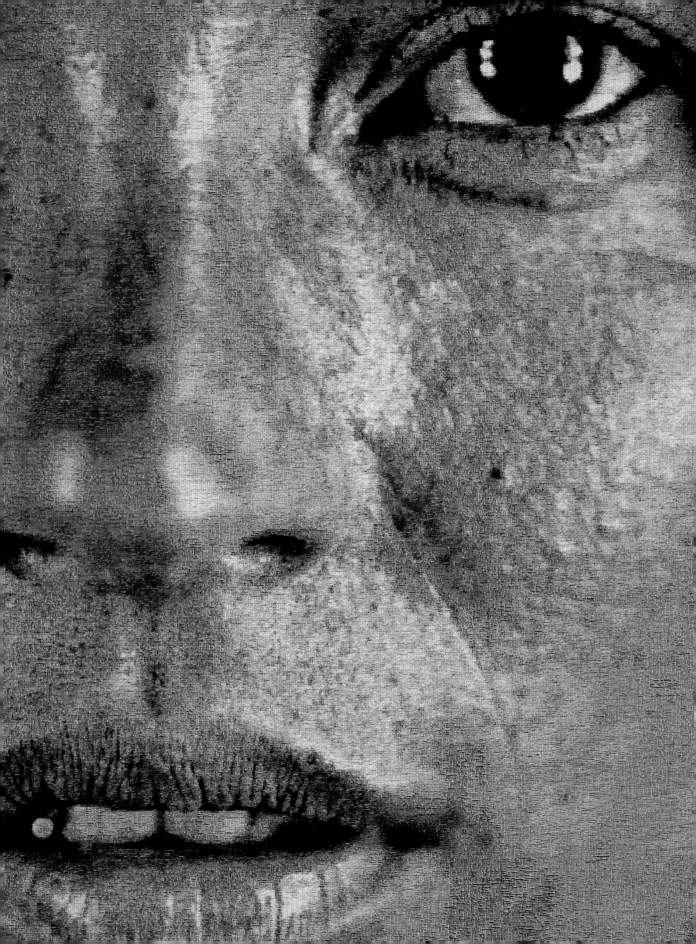

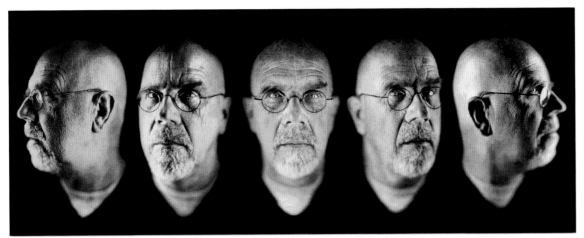

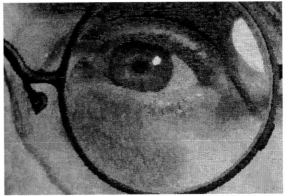

ABOVE
Chuck Close, *Self-Portrait/Five Part* (top), 2009. State I:
191 × 470 cm (75 × 185 in.); state II: 201 × 582 cm (79 × 229 in.);
Chuck Close, *Self-Portrait/Color* (bottom), 2007, 262 ×
201 cm (103 × 79 in.), Jacquard tapestries in archival cottons
and viscose

OPPOSITE
Chuck Close, *Kate* (detail), 2007, 262 × 201 cm (103 × 79 in.),
Jacquard tapestry in archival cottons and viscose

'The use of digital tools and process has enabled my practice to work beyond the material world, and push new boundaries of the perceived limitations of the hand and eye. These intangible tools sit alongside my traditional workbench, as it is this synergy that leads to unexpected explorations of material and form.'

GEOFFREY MANN

VISUALIZING INTANGIBLE FORCES IN TRADITIONAL CRAFTSMANSHIP

ABOVE
Cross-Fire, 2010, from the *Natural Occurrence* series

OPPOSITE
Shine (top left), 2005–10, bronze cast and silver-plated candelabra, from the *Natural Occurrence* series; *Cross-Fire* (top right and bottom left); *Attracted to Light* (bottom right), from the *Long Exposure* series

Artist and designer Geoffrey Mann explores his fascination with capturing the ephemeral nature of time and motion by applying a range of digital technologies, along with traditional craftsmanship, to his practice. His now iconic homeware for the *Natural Occurrence* series demonstrates how he takes everyday objects and subverts them by applying virtual forces to a digital model, before freezing the split-second reaction and crafting the moment as the finished piece.

Part of the series is the *Cross-Fire* collection (left), a physical manifestation of the usually intangible characteristics of sound waves, and their effect on the environment through which they travel. Mann recorded samples of the clashing sounds of a dinner-table argument (from the film *American Beauty*) and visualized the deforming effect the sounds might have on the inanimate objects on the table. A digital model of each transformed object – teapot, cutlery, wine glass – was turned into a mould using rapid-prototyping, from which the final pieces were cast.

For *Shine* (opposite, top left), Mann investigated the reflective properties of a silver candelabra by creating a digital model of the light rays bouncing off the surface using a planar 3D-scanner, the intensity of the reflections represented by the spikes. This three-dimensional embodiment of the sparkling light effect was 3D-printed and cast in bronze, using the lost-wax method, and plated in silver.

For *Attracted To Light* (opposite, bottom right), from his *Long Exposure* series, Mann used cinematic motion technology to capture the blur of a moth flying around a light source and translated it into a three-dimensional form, which was then sculpted in laser-sintered nylon.

LOCATION EDINBURGH, UK **TECHNIQUES** CAD-MODELLING, 3D-SCANNING, SELECTIVE LASER-SINTERING, TRADITIONAL CASTING **MATERIALS** NYLON, CERAMIC, GLASS, WAX, BRONZE, SILVER **WEBSITE** MRMANN.CO.UK

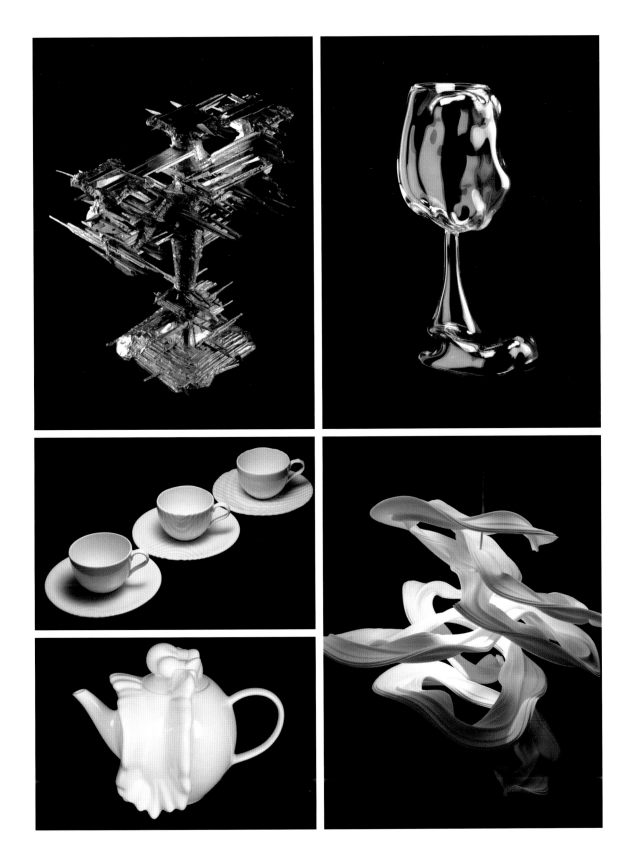

'In a fast-moving world this lamp is already
a piece of history. But I think that is the reason
why it is interesting now. I have always been
interested in designing for the specific moment
– the moment when a technique is already
available but not yet known by a broad public.'

LUC
MERX

A MONUMENTAL MASTERPIECE
FOR THE MODERN AGE

OPPOSITE
Fall of the Damned, 2006,
private collection; limited
editions available from
mgxbymaterialise.com

The creation of this extraordinary, intricate chandelier was inspired
by Peter Paul Rubens's masterpiece *The Fall of the Damned*, painted
in 1620. Depicting a mass of writhing, tumbling bodies, the circular
structure was produced using the selective laser-sintering technique
in polyamide nylon, which allowed for the complex under-cuttings and
overhanging parts, and would not have been possible by any other
production process.

It was printed as a single piece on the largest SLS machine available
at the time. The form was computer-modelled in Cinema 4D, comprising
twelve groups of seventeen bodies, which all rotate around the vertical
central axis. To avoid the need for an additional supporting structure,
the volume of each body just touches the next, fusing the whole design
together. The original work, from a limited edition of forty, is in the
private collection of pioneering 3D-printing production studio MGX.

LOCATION AACHEN, GERMANY **PROJECT** *FALL OF THE
DAMNED* (2006) **TECHNIQUES** 3D-MODELLING SOFTWARE,
ADDITIVE LAYER MANUFACTURING **MATERIALS** POLYAMIDE
NYLON **DIMENSIONS** 63 × 27 CM (25 × 11 IN.); 15 KG (33 LBS)
WEBSITE ROKOKORELEVANZ.DE

ABOVE
The final drawings for the chandelier,
viewed from below and from the side

OPPOSITE
Details of the original chandelier

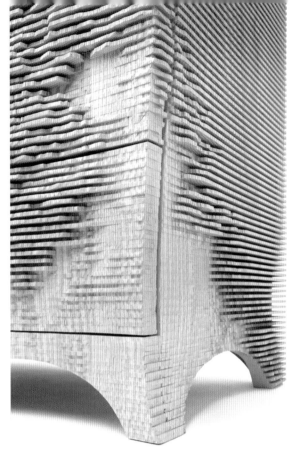

THIS PAGE
Three Drawer George, 2008, rectilinear commode,
CNC-routed in ash wood

OPPOSITE
Anne (top), 2007, pair of rectilinear chairs, CNC-
routed in American walnut; *Vessels* (bottom), 2009,
floor-standing sculptures, CNC-routed in ash wood

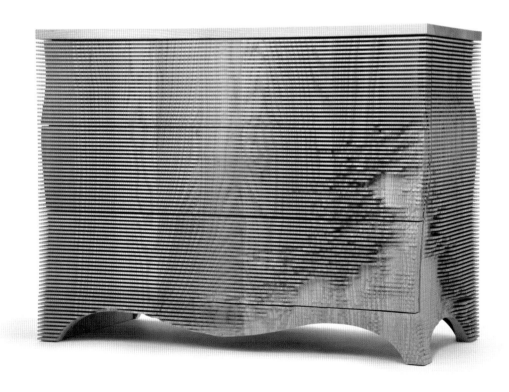

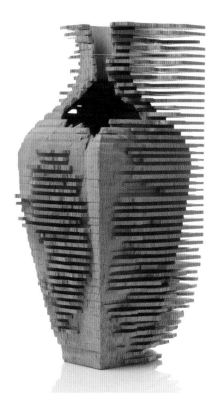

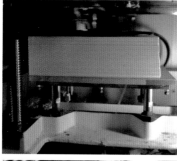

THESE PAGES
Lacquered Paper Objects, 2012, limited-edition collection

ABOVE
The pots are carefully broken free from the paper block,
before being lacquered by hand

NERVOUS SYSTEM

BIOMIMETIC CREATIONS FREED FROM THE CONSTRAINTS OF NATURE

Design studio Nervous System pioneers an emerging aesthetic that unites science, technology and art, using digital-fabrication methods to do justice to the precision of their designs. The team uses proprietary computer-simulation techniques to sculpt works that mimic the structural growth processes of organic forms. Using custom-built algorithmic software, the complex structure of each piece is uniquely generated, as in nature, so that no two are ever exactly alike.

Most of the pieces are printed using the laser-sintering method in polyamide nylon, which is then dyed, while works in silver are cast from 3D-printed wax models, using the lost-wax method. A recent collection, *Colony* (p. 173), explores the potential of multi-colour laser-sintered printing. The *Hyphae* collection of jewelry and homeware (opposite) features a textured construction generated by simulating the structures of biological circulatory systems, mimicking the growth of veins in leaves or animals. Beginning with a seed and a surface, the software 'grows' a hierarchical network that branches and interconnects.

Formed from a different simulation and production method, the *Folium* collection (p. 172) is the result of a digital growth process devised by the studio that mimics the growth of algae. Each design represents a specimen of a hypothetical new plant species; freed from the constraints of biology and physics, the pieces exhibit forms and patterns that would be impossible in nature. Every piece is a one-off, photochemically etched from stainless steel to achieve precise detail, and presented with a unique series number.

LOCATION SOMERVILLE, MASSACHUSETTS, USA
TECHNIQUES CAD-MODELLING, LASER-SINTERING, 3D-PRINTING, LOST-WAX METHOD, PHOTOCHEMICAL ETCHING **MATERIALS** POLYAMIDE NYLON, STAINLESS STEEL, SILVER **WEBSITE** N-E-R-V-O-U-S.COM

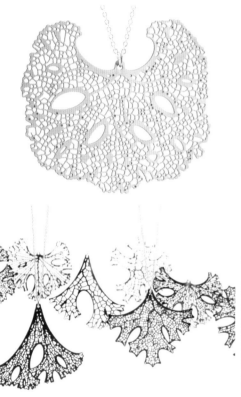

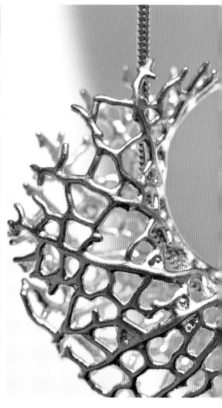

ABOVE
Folium, 2013, a series of uniquely generated pendants, photochemically etched in stainless steel

ABOVE AND RIGHT
Vessel pendant, 2011, 3D-printed polyamide nylon and cast silver, and *Spiral* cuff, 2007, 3D-printed in polyamide nylon

'We create simulations that grow forms based on a set of rules we program. We don't think of these simulations merely as tools, we think of them as our medium. Our choice to use digital fabrication is a natural one for us; it's the only option that makes sense. We are freed to invest our time in creating new ways to generate form.'

THIS PAGE
Colony, 2013, multi-colour laser-sintering in dyed polyamide nylon

'Digital fabrication is, in many ways, very restrictive, so it is important to consider those machines as just one tool, and not the only way of making. I really enjoy combining hand-skills alongside any digital tool I might choose to use, to give my products individual attention during their construction.'

ELAINE YAN LING NG

THE CREATIVITY OF ARTIFICIAL MATERIAL ENGINEERING

With both a scientific and creative education, textile designer and artist Elaine Yan Ling Ng explores the relationships between material characteristics and structural forms through experimental accessories, textiles and art installations. The installation *Naturology* (opposite top and p. 178) uses artificial material technology to simulate the movements of biological constructions in response to atmospheric conditions.

Ng has developed bespoke shape-memory materials that react to changes in temperature and humidity – contracting and curling or expanding and flattening out accordingly. Each piece begins as a flat combination of precisely laser-cut veneers and textiles – for accuracy, to ensure unrestricted movement between surfaces – and aesthetic handcrafted details and pivoting elements, which are too sensitive for a machine. Then, once the piece is exposed to rising levels of humidity and temperature – if hung outside, for example – the materials begin to respond to their surroundings, contracting and curling to form baubles.

For *Climatology*, Ng continued her research into smart textiles and the self-adapting engineering of plant structures, such as pinecones. For this collection of accessories, layers of laser-cut and etched wood veneers and fabrics, with reactive dyes and reflective surfaces, are shaped into rings, neck pieces and hair ornaments – which gently unfurl, responding to light and heat and moving together in harmony with the wearer's environment.

OPPOSITE
Headpiece from the *Climatology* collection (top); flat elements from the *Naturology* collection (bottom), before unfurling in response to their environment

LOCATION HONG KONG, CHINA **TECHNIQUES** GRAPHIC SOFTWARE, LASER-CUTTING, LASER-ETCHING, EMBROIDERY, HAND-FINISHING **MATERIALS** SHAPE MEMORY ALLOY, SHAPE MEMORY FIBRE, SMART VENEERS, THREADS **WEBSITE** ELAINEYANLINGNG.COM

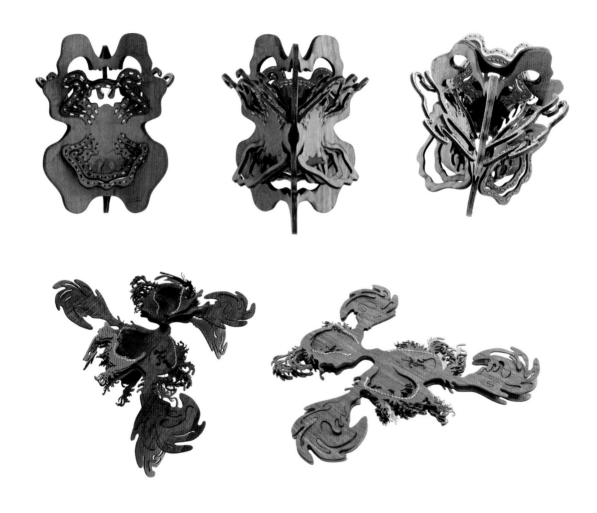

ABOVE
The unfurling process of a piece from the *Naturology*
collection (top); a ring from the *Climatology*
accessories collection (bottom)

OPPOSITE
A ring (top) and shoulder piece (bottom) from the
Climatology accessories collection

NERI OXMAN

THE INTERSECTION OF MATERIAL ENGINEERING AND ECOLOGY

As founder of the Mediated Matter research group at MIT Media Lab, Neri Oxman is dedicated to enhancing the relationship between manmade and natural environments through the application of advanced fabrication tools and technologies to the making of architectural, furniture and wearable forms.

Beast (overleaf), from a series exploring 'material ecology', is a prototype for a sculptural chaise longue, and was created by the application of form-generation protocols that mimic the streamlined shapes found in nature. Using multi-material 3D-printing technology, it was fabricated as a single, flowing shape, with opacity and colour varied to achieve an intriguing pattern of light and shade. Oxman's designs for the *Arache* corset, featuring a web of flexible cells, and the *Medusa 2* helmet (above), an investigation into the processes of perforation, corrugation and wrinkling, push the limits of multi-colour 3D-printing.

A recent work, *Gemini Acoustic Chaise* (opposite), combines this printing process with CNC-milling, and pairs synthetic and natural materials, hard and soft sensations, additive and subtractive fabrication. The textured skin is made of a sound-absorbing elastic material, the first design to use forty-four different materials in Stratasys's Connex3 3D-printing process, which features preset mechanical combinations to vary the rigidity, opacity and colour. The surface 'cells' deflect and absorb surrounding sounds, while offering a comfortable chair to sit on.

LOCATION CAMBRIDGE, MASSACHUSETTS, USA **TECHNIQUES** CAD-MODELLING, MULTI-MATERIAL 3D-PRINTING **MATERIALS** VARIOUS RIGID AND RUBBER COMPOSITES **WEBSITE** NERI.MEDIA.MIT.EDU

'The incredible design possibilities afforded by multi-material bitmap printing allow us to reinterpret the age-old tradition of dithering, practiced in the printed press industry, as well as in textile crafts, and replace complex delicate manual labour with code. The level of detail and material resolution opens new possibilities for designers.'

THESE PAGES
Beast, 2008–10, prototype chaise longue,
3D-printed with Stratasys multi-material technology

'I prefer to spend a day in a workshop, rather than in front of my computer. But new technologies help us work better and faster to create things that never existed before. We need both disciplines to keep making our surroundings an inspiring place to be in.'

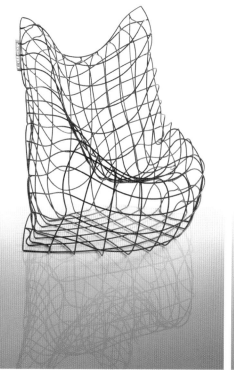

THESE PAGES
Left to right:
Fatboy; *Red Blue*; *Louis*; *Kubus*, all from the *Icons* series, 2011, based on classic chair designs

In a process of 'reverse engineering', furniture designer Jan Plechác created the *Icons* series of chairs, based on a corresponding series of historic chair designs. First, a CAD model of each chair was made, accurately reproducing each form as a three-dimensional wireframe. Plechác then refined each of these models, gradually reducing the individual lines of the mesh until he was left with the minimum number of lines required to sketch a clearly recognizable outline of each chair.

Using a thin steel rod to represent each sketched line, he then carefully hand-formed a physical, full-scale version of each chair. The digital drawing provided a reference for the exact lengths and bent dimensions of each rod, which Plechác welded into place at the precisely defined crossing points.

The final structure of each chair was then painted black, to further resemble the original digital wireframe sketch. It also plays a trick on the eye, which does not expect to see this digital aesthetic actually come to life in a tactile, three-dimensional form. The *Icons* series won a Czech Grand Design Award in 2011.

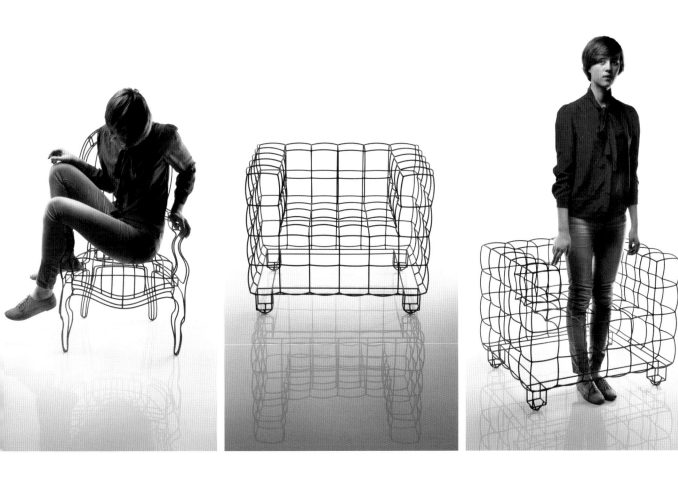

JAN PLECHÁC

SKETCHING HISTORICAL DESIGNS IN THREE DIMENSIONS

LOCATION PRAGUE, CZECH REPUBLIC **TECHNIQUES** CAD-MODELLING, METAL BENDING AND WELDING **MATERIALS** STEEL, PAINT **WEBSITE** JANANDHENRY.COM

'Digital tools require the learning of new skills, but don't necessarily replace or make redundant traditional hand-skills. With 3D-printing, new visual languages emerge that are worth exploring.'

MATTHEW PLUMMER-FERNANDEZ

DISRUPTIVE EXPRESSIONS OF OUR DIGITIZED SOCIETY

THESE PAGES
sekuMoi Mecy, 2012,
3D-printed in plaster powder
and coloured inks

Artist and designer Matthew Plummer-Fernandez expresses his fascination with artificial intelligence and the fall-out from our digitized society by developing distinctive digital translation and fabrication processes. In an early work, *Glitch Reality I* (p. 189), he 3D-scanned a sporting trophy, enlarging the resulting digital model to human scale, and CNC-milled the form from a block of foam.

These explorations led to the series *Digital Natives* (p. 188), in which everyday household items were 3D-scanned and converted into digital models, and subjected to a series of distorting software algorithms, before the application of a graduating colour palette. The final forms were 3D-printed in colour, using the additive layer manufacturing technique with a plaster powder and coloured inks, and sealed with a hand-applied transparent adhesive skin.

With *sekuMoi Mecy* (these pages; an anagram of Mickey Mouse), Plummer-Fernandez further explored the derivatives of the 3D-scanning process. Here, he took an icon of commercial culture, and again applied algorithms to deform the resulting copy, before altering the colours to fit the faceted form and 3D-printing it in plaster.

A similar process was used for *Venus of Google* (p. 189), generated from an original image found on Google of a model draped in a pose reminiscent of the classic image of Venus. It was subjected to deforming algorithms, this time gradually building up a volume around the two-dimensional picture, which in turn was 3D-printed in coloured plaster.

LOCATION LONDON, UK **TECHNIQUES** 3D-SCANNING, CAD-MODELLING, 3D-PRINTING, HAND-FINISHING **MATERIALS** PLASTER, DYE, ADHESIVE
WEBSITE PLUMMERFERNANDEZ.COM

ABOVE
sekuMoi Mecy 3 (left), 2013, and *Venus of Google*
(top right), 2013, both 3D-printed in plaster powder
and coloured inks; *Glitch Reality I* (bottom right),
2010, CNC-milled from foam

OPPOSITE
Digital Natives, 2012, 3D-printed sculptures
from 3D-scans of everyday objects

'Machine collaboration is something new in the world and the new possibilities signal an exciting time. The human desire to recreate its own image, coupled with these developing technologies, is expanding possibilities for sculpture and art as a whole.'

LOUIS PRATT

MODERN DIGITAL DEPENDENCE MADE PHYSICAL

Louis Pratt, one of the first artists in Australia to build an open-source Rapman 3D-printer, creates sculptural expressions that are enmeshed with digital tools. They also imagine, to striking effect, the physical impact of the human figure being subjected to the rules of the cyber world and digital data.

Pratt's sculpture, *Yea, I Know* (opposite, bottom), explores how the mathematical sine wave can be applied to a three-dimensional form and the dimensions of the figure resolved to still be perceived as normally proportioned, when viewed from a certain angle. Another work, *Virus* (opposite, top), distorts the organic data using Boolean functions to delete parts of the digital model, before it is physically built.

In all of Pratt's works, the process begins by scanning a model to create a set of organic data points (unlike inorganic data, which is only produced inside software). The data is manipulated with algorithmic software to create the final distorted forms, before being prepared for 3D-printing. Each sculpture is printed in multiple pieces, using thermal plastic printers, and assembled and finished with sanding and painting. Even using two high-definition 3D-printers to accelerate the process, most of Pratt's larger works take a minimum of 800 hours to print.

Works such as *Yea, I Know* are finished as a 3D print, while others are cast in bronze, through the traditional lost-wax method, using the 3D print as the model.

LOCATION SYDNEY, AUSTRALIA **TECHNIQUES** CAD SOFTWARE, 3D-PRINTING, BRONZE CASTING **MATERIALS** POLYLACTIDE, BRONZE **WEBSITE** LOUISPRATT.COM

'I approach working with the computer as if it is an extension of my hand. Although I like that it helps me be more structured and precise, it is important that my creative process is still grounded in human skill and a true feeling for the subjects.'

ABOVE
Molotov-cocktail, 2012, mixed textiles

OPPOSITE
Tomas and the House of Ask, 2013, mixed textiles

CÉDRIC RAGOT

HISTORIC AND NATURAL FORMS WITH A TECHNOLOGICAL TWIST

Hyper Fast Vase (p. 204) was Cédric Ragot's first experience of using software to capture movement in a three-dimensional, static form. This now iconic family of vases originated with a digital model of the archetypal shape of a Ming vase, which was subjected to the forces of digital acceleration and frozen in time – the smooth form of each blur then painstakingly rendered. The final vase was produced through a complex process of 3D-printed mould-making and traditional casting, glazing and firing, allowing only a limited number of copies to be made.

A later work, *Palm Vase*, created for Italian ceramics manufacturer Bitossi Ceramiche, was an experiment in transitioning between volume and surface to present an object that is stable but gives the illusion of growing. Ragot first modelled the form in CAD, before 3D-printing a prototype from which moulds were made for casting less than two hundred limited-edition pieces.

For the biomorphic *La Chose* (p. 205), the flowing surfaces were created using 3-axis CNC-milling; the machine could only carve depths of up to 5 cm (2 in.), so the original prototype for the chair was formed from a series of carved wooden layers assembled by hand. The final collection of stools was then cast in fibreglass and polyester resin.

For the lighting installation *13,000 Volts* (these pages), Ragot modelled the convolutions of the brain directly into CAD, from which a model of the negative volume was extracted. This negative of the brain shape was then 3D-printed, to form a solid mould into which the glass blower laid the glass tube lighting to build up the final sculptural form.

THESE PAGES
13,000 Volts, 2010,
illuminated glass sculpture

LOCATION MONTREUIL, FRANCE **TECHNIQUES** CAD-MODELLING, 3D-PRINTING, CNC-MILLING, CERAMIC CASTING **MATERIALS** PORCELAIN, GLASS, FIBREGLASS, POLYESTER RESIN **WEBSITE** CEDRICRAGOT.COM

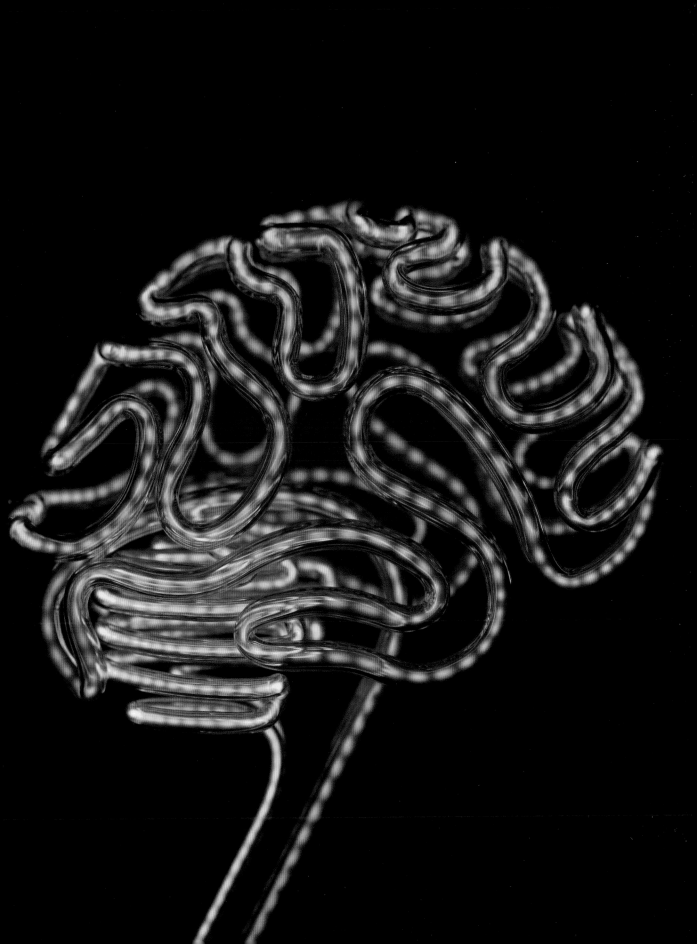

'I am constantly fascinated by the manufacturing process. I love experimenting in new fields, new materials. The way materials are transformed and assembled. I don't like to specialize. Inspiration can come from everything or anywhere.'

ABOVE
Hyper Fast Vase, 2003, cast in porcelain from a 3D-printed mould

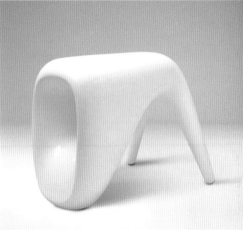

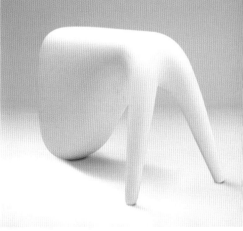

ABOVE
La Chose, 2003, fibreglass and resin,
cast from a 3-axis milled wooden mould

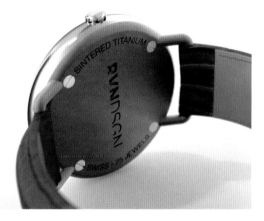

ZACH RAVEN

PERFECTING THE INDUSTRIAL FABRICATION OF TIME

OPPOSITE
RVNDSGN collection, 2011, with 3D-printed cases Clockwise from top left: black anodized brushed titanium; polished titanium; raw sintered titanium; polished titanium with metal wrist strap

Industrial designer Zach Raven has recently turned his attention to exploring the capabilities of 3D-printing as a solution for offering one-off, high-quality products to the market at an accessible price. What began as an experiment has evolved quickly to become the sophisticated, boutique line of *RVNDSGN* titanium watches, launched in 2011.

The fabrication process employs the technique of selective laser-sintering, with stainless steel for the watch faces and solid titanium for the cases. Each timepiece is printed and assembled to order, allowing the client to choose a combination of colour, face design and style of strap. After a number of early prototypes with acrylic elements proved popular, the workshop launched a new, refined design, offered with a polished titanium case, a black anodized brushed version or a sintered version, which retains the grain from the 3D-printing process.

The internal workings of each hand-assembled piece feature the highest-quality components, including a scratch-proof sapphire watch crystal, twenty-five-jewel Swiss mechanical automatic movement – ensuring the watch keeps itself wound, no battery required – and alligator-grain leather or titanium straps.

LOCATION GRAND RAPIDS, MICHIGAN, USA
TECHNIQUES LASER-SINTERING, HAND-FINISHING
MATERIALS TITANIUM, STAINLESS STEEL
WEBSITE RVNDSGN.COM

'The joy of this process is that every product is unique to its owner, and we are constantly surprised by the tiny textural details that result from the sintering process. We feel that retaining these marks adds to the pleasure of wearing a piece like this.'

'I am fascinated by how we can capture memories, and how digital technologies reshape design and our relationship with the world we live in. Good design should tell a good story, and digital tools are enabling us to faithfully capture more of these stories of our lives.'

GUTO REQUENA

INVISIBLE IMPRESSIONS MADE MANIFEST THROUGH CRAFTSMANSHIP

THESE PAGES
Nóize Chairs, 2012, 3D-printed in ABS thermoplastic from a computer model disrupted by sound waves

Multi-disciplinary designer Guto Requena brings together the worlds of technology and traditional craft in his beautiful and unusual designs. For the *Era Uma Vez* collection of glass vases (p. 210), he recorded his grandmother reading four favourite childhood stories. The sound waves generated were translated into a 2D digital graphic, which was rotated around a vertical axis to shape the 3D cylindrical object. This volume was rapid-prototyped in polyamide nylon and used to make an iron mould, into which the glass for the final vases was blown.

Nóize Chairs (these pages) was a study in capturing the urban sounds of São Paulo and merging them with the shapes of iconic chair designs, which were faithfully reproduced in CAD, and merged into a single composite chair form. The digital soundscape was then applied to disrupt the model, creating a final structure that displays the sonic interference across its surfaces. The chair was 3D-printed in black ABS thermoplastic, using the fused deposition modelling technique.

For the *Losing My America* project, initiated by GT2P (p. 90), Requena created *Nossa Senhora Des-Aparecida* (p. 211), collaborating with craftsmen from Sutaco, a community of artisans in São Paulo. A wooden statue was cut in half down the centre, and the right section reconstructed in polyamide nylon using the technique of stereolithography, modelled from abstracted 3D scans of the original work. The final piece was then coated in a copper shower.

LOCATION SÃO PAULO, BRAZIL **TECHNIQUES** CAD-MODELLING, AUDIO CAPTURE, GLASS BLOWING, FUSED DEPOSITION MODELLING, STEREOLITHOGRAPHY **MATERIALS** GLASS, ABS THERMOPLASTIC, POLYAMIDE NYLON, WOOD, COPPER **WEBSITE** GUTOREQUENA.COM.BR

ABOVE
Era Uma Vez (Once Upon a Time), 2011.
From left: *The Dove and the Ant*;
The Wren and the Owl; *A Party in Heaven*

OPPOSITE
Nossa Senhora Des-Aparecida, 2014,
created for the *Losing My America* project

'Being able to design my own audio visualization software specifically for digital weaving has opened doors and encouraged me to learn a new creative language. Quite simply, BeatWoven exists because of the digital tools involved.'

NADIA-ANNE RICKETTS

THE WEAVING OF MUSIC IN VISUAL FORM

Multi-media textile designer Nadia-Anne Ricketts begins each project by uploading a piece of music to her proprietary BeatWoven software. This process enables her to visualize the digital pattern generated, and to explore the emotive qualities of the music through colours and textures, considering the final application of the fabric in the choice of materials.

Once the relationship between the music, materials and details of the pattern are understood visually, either the entire piece or a section of the music will be used, depending on the desired look of the final textile. Ricketts then works through the digital pattern in detail, hand-editing it to prepare the weave file for the loom. Doing so allows her to extract and develop repeating patterns, playing with composition, scale and colour to give more variety and depth to the design.

Having finalized the design, she then allocates colours and textures to build up the weave structure. Before weaving the final design, she samples parts of it on the loom, balancing the proportions of the pattern with the yarns and structures being applied, making alterations by hand to ensure that the resulting rhythms of the textile surface represent accurately the timing of the original piece of music.

Ricketts has created textiles based on musical genres ranging from lullabies to dubstep to classical – including, most recently, a large-scale permanent work for the Royal Festival Hall, in London, based on Rachmaninov's Piano Concerto No. 2.

LOCATION LONDON, UK **TECHNIQUES** AUDIO-VISUALIZATION SOFTWARE, DIGITAL JACQUARD WEAVING **MATERIALS** SILK, COTTON, WOOL AND METALLIC YARNS **WEBSITE** BEATWOVEN.CO.UK

'In countries like Mexico there is a natural co-existence between design and craft culture. Digital technologies can fit into our creative methodologies without friction if we respect the skills and values of both worlds.'

ARIEL ROJO

HARMONIES ACROSS DIGITAL TECHNOLOGY AND CRAFT CULTURE

Almost all the output from Ariel Rojo's wide-ranging design studio combines digital modelling and fabrication techniques with a celebration of the traditions of craft culture in his native Mexico and beyond. An early design piece, the energy-efficient *Saving Pig Lamp* (p. 216), was CAD-modelled and a mould 3D-printed, before being crafted in stoneware and finished with glazes, including limited-edition Talavera decoration.

For the eye-catching *Foco Rojo* rug (opposite), Rojo took a digital satellite image of Mexico City's dense urban sprawl and translated the intensities into a detailed, abstracted pattern, with each pixel representing a strand of wool. The final piece was handmade in India by Odabashian Rugs for the Mario Friedmann Gallery, London. And for his *Al-ma* collection of street furniture (p. 216), prototypes were CNC-milled in MDF for precision, before the final pieces were sand-cast in 100 per cent recycled aluminium and coated in electrostatic paint.

As a contribution to the cultural project *Losing My America*, initiated by GT2P (p. 90), Rojo created the *Talavera* jug (p. 216) and *Huichol* skull (p. 217), both of which were studies of the effects of digitizing traditional Mexican decorative techniques. Each involved 3D-scanning original objects, which were then manipulated and the pixellated effects exaggerated, before being 3D-printed in ABS plastic and cast in clay. The pieces were then hand-decorated, half in a traditional style and half with a digitized aesthetic – the jug with painted Talavera decoration and the skull with tiny glass beads reflecting the art of the Huichol people.

OPPOSITE
Foco Rojo, 2013, handmade woven rug, based on digital satellite images of Mexico City

LOCATION MEXICO CITY, MEXICO **TECHNIQUES** CAD-MODELLING, GRAPHIC SOFTWARE, 3D-PRINTING, CLAY CASTING, HAND-WEAVING, CNC-MILLING **MATERIALS** STONEWARE, WOOL, ALUMINIUM, CLAY, ABS PLASTIC **WEBSITE** ARIELROJO.COM

ABOVE
Clockwise from top left:
Al-ma, 2013, from a collection of street furniture,
sand cast from recycled aluminium; *Talavera* jug, 2014,
from the *Losing My America* collection; *Saving Pig Lamp*,
2008, both cast in clay from a 3D-printed mould and
decorated in the Talavera style

OPPOSITE
Huichol skull, 2014, from the *Losing My America* collection,
cast in clay from a 3D-printed mould and decorated with
glass beads

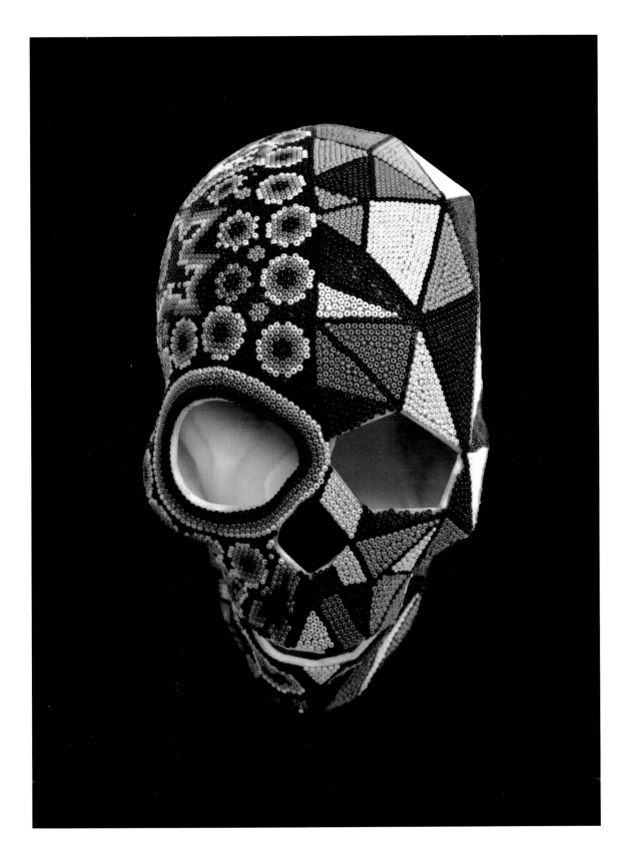

'Digital tools are like any other tool. When used appropriately they can improve the execution of an idea, but when used inappropriately they can have the opposite effect. For me, they offer the potential of pushing the boundaries of the possible.'

THIS PAGE
The original models of each element are made in resin, using the technique of stereolithography to obtain a high level of detail

OPPOSITE
Cuff links in gold and platinum (top), and a raw cast of a gold pen casing (bottom), removed from its supportive structure, both from the *Architect* collection

'I don't believe digital technologies will replace traditional handcraft. What is most exciting to me is the intersection between the two. From my perspective, it will be the combination of human gesture and machine gesture that will produce the most creative work.'

LIN STANIOUS

NATURAL FORM MEETS TECHNOLOGICAL FUNCTION

Lin Stanionis's jewelry designs are testament to a highly skilled exploration of the intersection between digital fabrication and traditional craftsmanship. Each work is labour intensive, involving a number of technical processes to produce the finished product. While a number of digitally controlled tools are used to machine various parts, these are then employed to create rubber moulds for casting and do not appear as elements in the final piece.

Each design starts with an object from nature – such as a rattlesnake head or the claws of a bird – or a model made in wax. While Stanionis sculpts many details by hand, some of the more geometric elements, including the rippling centre of *Rosepool* (overleaf) and the oval frame in *Rapture* (p. 225), are sculpted digitally and then carved in wax using the process of CNC-milling to capture the desired sharp, perfect detail.

These natural and wax objects are used to produce rubber moulds, from which final resin versions are cast. The cast-resin parts are then assembled – each piece of jewelry combining between eight and twelve separate pieces, all hand-polished to finish. In the pendant entitled *Confessional*, the five curved panels of the main body are similarly cast in resin in a silicone rubber mould made from an original piece carved in wax using a CNC mill.

THESE PAGES
Confessional, cast in resin in silicone moulds made from original CNC-milled and handmade wax elements

LOCATION OVERBROOK, KANSAS, USA **TECHNIQUES** CNC-MILLING, HAND-SCULPTING, TRADITIONAL MOULD-MAKING AND CASTING **MATERIALS** WAX, SILICONE RUBBER, URETHANE RESIN **WEBSITE** SNAGMETALSMITH.ORG/MEMBERS/LSTANIO

THESE PAGES
Rosepool (above, and opposite top and bottom right), and *Rapture* (bottom left), both cast in resin in silicone moulds made from original CNC-milled and handmade wax elements

ELISA STROZYK

A FLOWING QUILT WITH THE SCENT OF WOOD

Textile designer Elisa Strozyk's award-winning *Wooden Textiles* series introduces us to the character of wood in a new and surprising way – no longer hard and solid, but yielding, warm and sensuous. The results of her unique, mosaic-inspired technique are objects that are half-wood, half-textile – products that look and smell like wood, but, unexpectedly, flow like soft quilts. Strozyk maps out the patterns using software, or simply works them out by hand as she constructs each unique piece.

The signature small, triangular tiles of her designs – numbering in their thousands for each finished work – are laser-cut from thin sheets of natural or dyed wood veneer, before being individually hand-glued onto a cotton textile base. Laser-cutting allows Strozyk to prepare the many tiles she needs with speed and efficiency, as well as the geometric precision to produce the folding qualities necessary to achieve the tactility of the finished textiles.

The strength and flexibility of the finished designs allow them to function as blankets, carpets and even lampshades, all of which crumple neatly at the touch. The lampshades use single layers of translucent veneer, to allow maximum warmth of light, while the carpets might use multiple layers of veneer to build up a robust surface.

Strozyk also collaborated with Icelandic menswear designer Sruli Recht on his *Concentrated* collection, Autumn/Winter 2013, which featured a striking coat and chunky jumper made from pure black and white versions of her wooden textiles.

OPPOSITE
A multi-coloured, patterned composition from the award-winning *Wooden Textiles* range, 2009–ongoing

LOCATION HAMBURG, GERMANY **TECHNIQUES** GRAPHIC SOFTWARE, LASER-CUTTING, HAND-FINISHING **WEBSITE** ELISASTROZYK.DE

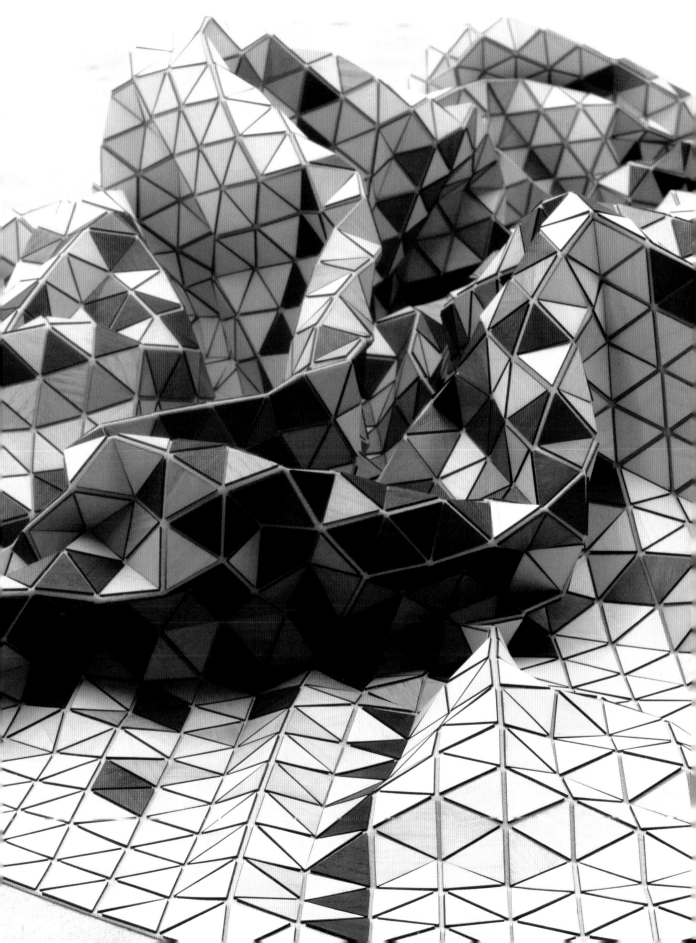

ABOVE
A patterned rug from the
Wooden Textiles collection

'The sense of touch is fundamental to my making process, so I need to work with my hands and feel the material. Still, I appreciate the endless possibilities of new digital technologies, and like to use them to realize creations which couldn't otherwise be made by human hands.'

ABOVE
Individual triangles for each design are laser-cut from sheets of wood veneer (left); a wooden jumper (right), produced with Sruli Recht for his *Concentrated* collection, Autumn/Winter 2013

LASZLO TOMPA

THE GEOMETRIC PERFECTION OF NATURAL FORMS

Remaining true to the qualities and values of traditional woodcraft, Laszlo Tompa subtly introduces digital design and fabrication processes into his work to help bring his geometrically perfect designs to life, and to the highest standards.

His celebrated storage box, *Cube Illusion* (p. 233), measuring 40 cm^2 (16 sq. in.), appears to be carved out of one block of wood – a complex construction of curves creating an optical illusion, with no visible straight lines to distinguish between the lid and the body of the box. Although the prototype was CNC-milled from multiple angles as a single, complete three-dimensional object, the resulting commercial design is constructed from an intricate assembly of individual smaller revolutions – each carved with a rotational lathe, to an exact two-dimensional template, laser-cut in steel. These separate revolutions are then fitted together by hand, and fixed onto a rectilinear inner box construction.

Following the success of the concept, Tompa expanded into lamps, creating the *Flower* (opposite and p. 232) and *Hydro* (p. 232) collections, inspired by botanical and maritime forms, respectively. As with all of Tompa's designs, the creation process for each lamp begins by constructing a digital model, from which a two-dimensional profile of each detail is extracted to create the lathe templates for carving a series of identical, precise rotational elements. These elements form the ornamental casing for an internal hexagonal or pentagonal framework.

OPPOSITE
Lamps from the *Flower* collection, 2014, cherry wood, created on a rotational lathe to a CNC-milled design

LOCATION ZSÁMBÉK, HUNGARY **TECHNIQUES** CAD-MODELLING, LASER-CUTTING, CNC-MILLING, ROTATIONAL LATHING
MATERIALS SOLID CHERRY **WEBSITE** TOMPAKERAMIA.HU

'For me, the computer is the same tool as the pencil. It opens the door to simulation of several ideas in a short time, so I can find the best route more quickly. Digital design and traditional hand-skills are combined in all of my works, to create novel and original forms.'

ABOVE
Lamps from the *Flower* (top left) and *Hydro* (bottom left and right) collections, both 2014

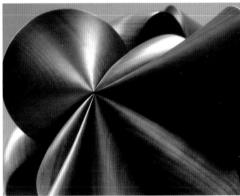

THIS PAGE
Cube Illusion, 2011, cherry wood,
created on a rotational lathe to
a CNC-milled design

'Tools have always been used as an extension to the hand. Now, aspects of the pre-industrial craft economy merge with high-tech industrial production methods, with the potential to shift power from producers to the designer and the consumer.'

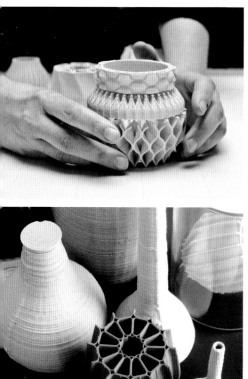

ABOVE
The Peddler, 2013,
orange clay diffuser

OPPOSITE
Stratigraphic Porcelain,
carafe and tumblers,
3D-printed in layers of clay

Unfold is at the forefront of the exploration of 3D-printed ceramics, using a specially developed open-source RepRap 3D-printer to lay down thin lines of clay and directly shape the object. Early in their research phase, the studio introduced the installation *L'Artisan Electronique*, in which the printer is combined with digital-modelling technologies and movement sensors to allow users to 'model' a vessel with hand gestures on a virtual potter's wheel, before seeing the resulting digital image printed in clay.

For the evolving *Stratigraphic Porcelain* tableware series (opposite), each piece is assigned its own source code, referring to the unique combination of structural and textural elements featured in the design. Each printed object begins with the development of a digital model, amalgamating various structures and faceted elements that have been tested for printability, before being translated into clay.

Recently the studio created a bespoke collection of ceramic ware, based on this proven process, for *The Peddler* (above), an artisan perfume brand produced in collaboration with *parfumeur* Barnabé Fillion for Maison & Objet. Demonstrating the most refined version yet of the studio's 3D-printed ceramic technique, this series of perfume-making vessels possess a complex structure that provides additional surface area for the diffusion of the fragrances.

UNFOLD

INNOVATIVE INTERVENTIONS WITHIN
AN AGE-OLD CRAFT PROCESS

LOCATION ANTWERP, BELGIUM **TECHNIQUES** CAD-MODELLING, 3D
CERAMIC PRINTING **MATERIALS** PORCELAIN CLAY **WEBSITE** UNFOLD.BE

ABOVE
The Peddler, 2013, collection of tools and vessels

OPPOSITE
Unfold's customized RepRap 3D-printer, which prints
direct in clay extruded through the central nozzle

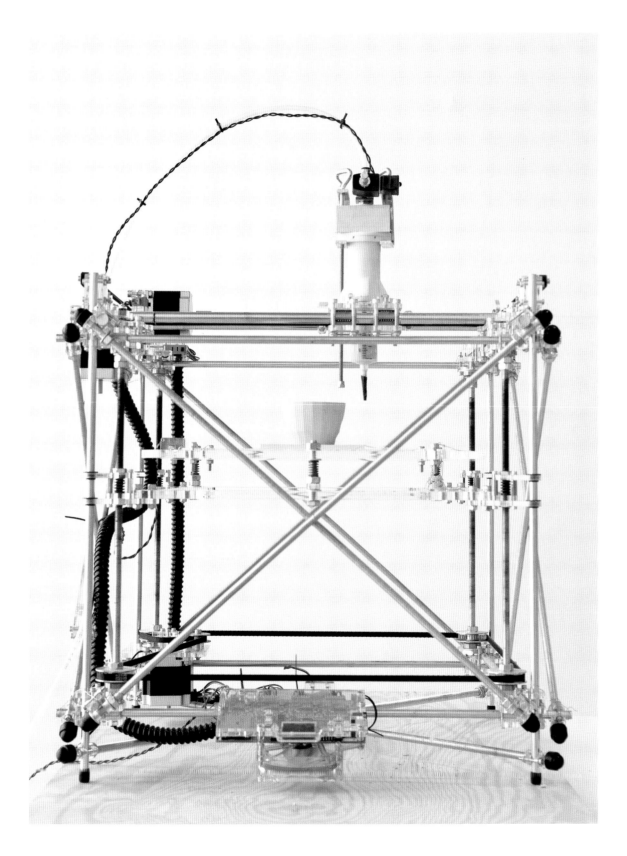

UUFIE

NATURAL SHOWMANSHIP, CAPTURED IN A MOMENT

'Both digital and traditional tools help expand our design possibilities – showing us beyond what we can imagine, without conflict between the two. But it is important how and when to use each – there is a right time for each.'

Architecture studio UUfie's design for the *Peacock Chair* is an experiment in combining digital modelling, thermoforming and hand-sculpting. Created from a single sheet of acrylic composite, and featuring a precise lattice structure, the chair's sculptural form is intended to capture a moment in the natural movement of a flower blossoming or the fanning of a bird's tail.

First, a digital model of the precise shape is designed, from which a reverse mould is made using CNC-milled plywood. A flat sheet of acrylic composite material is cut to size, and the closed slits for the lattice structure sliced into the sheet using a CNC machine. Then, using the process of thermoforming, the sheet is heated and transformed by hand, within the reverse mould, to create the final shape.

The material properties enable the sheet to be stretched, manipulated and sculpted – to open and display the lattice pattern – but only within a limited time frame, before the sheet cools and hardens, literally freezing a moment of movement in time. The result fuses structural strength and a delicate decorative quality in one coherent form. It is produced in three versions: as a large limited edition (opposite), and a smaller version in white or colours (p. 240), for indoor or outdoor use.

LOCATION TORONTO, CANADA **TECHNIQUES** 3D-MILLING, THERMOFORMING **MATERIALS** PLYWOOD, ACRYLIC COMPOSITE SHEETS **WEBSITE** UUFIE.COM

ABOVE
The smaller version of the
Peacock Chair, in turquoise
acrylic composite

DIRK VANDER KOOIJ

NEW PRODUCTION TECHNIQUES AS THE CREATIVE PROCESS

ABOVE
Endess Flow Rocking Chair,
2011, extruded recycled plastic,
from the *Endless Chairs* series

OPPOSITE
New Babylon Chair (top), 2013,
and various iterations of the
Changing Vase (bottom), 2013,
3D-printed in recycled plastics

Originally a graduation project, designer Dirk Vander Kooij's *Endless* production technique has since developed into the ongoing aesthetic of his work. After detailed CAD-modelling, objects and pieces of furniture are created using the extrusion method of 3D-printing, in which melted recycled plastic is squeezed through a large nozzle, with each thick strand sticking to the one before and cooling on contact with the air to rapidly become structurally solid.

His *Endless Chairs* series has become an icon of this process: a simple, structural design with current versions deliberately retaining the look of the early, low-resolution 'pulse structure', which resulted in slightly wavy lines as the plastic was squeezed through the nozzle. It took fifty-four prototypes of the rocking version of the chair before achieving a level of comfort the designer was happy with.

From these early chairs, Kooij progressed to applying the process to tables, lamps and ornamental pieces – always using recycled plastics to create unexpected, one-off colourways. The production method has also evolved to include a fine version of the extruded texture, as in the *New Babylon Chair* (opposite, top), as well as introducing smoothed surfaces for comfort, such as the rubber top of the *Fat Line Table* (p. 244).

And as a waste-conscious exercise while making the paint tube-inspired *Chubby Chair* (p. 244), when the extrusion machine changes colours and the nozzle spills out some material, the excess volume of plastic is used to make the *Chubby Coat Hanger* collection.

LOCATION ZAANDAM, NETHERLANDS **TECHNIQUES** CAD-MODELLING,
EXTRUSION 3D-PRINTING **MATERIALS** REUSED PLASTICS
WEBSITE DIRKVANDERKOOIJ.NL

ABOVE
Calculated Chaos Chair (left), 2011, 3D-printed from extruded
aluminium, then polished; *Satellite Lamp* (right), 2011,
3D-printed from extruded clear plastic

OPPOSITE
Endless Flow Dining Chairs, 2011, from the *Endless Chairs*
series, and a cross-legged *Fat Line Table*, 2013 (top);
Chubby Chair (bottom), 2012, in various colours, created
from thickly extruded plastic

'I find development of the new techniques
required to fabricate a new design just as
interesting as the new design itself. It requires
constant readjustment until the form appears
as it does in my mind.'

IRIS VAN HERPEN

INDUSTRIAL ALCHEMY REVOLUTIONIZES HAUTE COUTURE

Renowned for her revolutionary creations, Iris Van Herpen is recognized as a leading designer in the application of digital-fabrication technologies for fashion. Her ongoing collaborations with pioneers across the sectors of science, architecture and art, as well as the rapid-prototyping studios Stratasys and Materialise, have resulted in extraordinary designs that push the boundaries of the imaginable on the catwalk.

Her early explorations in 3D-printing culminated in the *Escapism* collection (p. 249), a series of lightweight, flexible armour-like dresses, sculpted from selective laser-sintered polyamide nylon. The subsequent *Wilderness Embodied* collection (left and opposite), for which she collaborated with Isaïe Bloch (p. 32), unveiled a more advanced application of 3D-printing, using stereolithography to sculpt a flesh-coloured resin composite into the texture of fur and embossed detailing. Another collection, *Voltage*, explored the effects of electricity on cellular and crystalline formations, again using rapid-prototyping in resin.

The creation of the ethereal 'water' dress (p. 249) for the *Crystallization* collection used high-speed digital photography to capture splashes of water. These split-second images then became a reference for sculpting a specially formulated acrylic material – heated with hot air guns and manipulated with pliers – to exactly mimic the formation of water droplets, frozen in time.

The shoes featured in each of Van Herpen's seasonal collections were conceived and 3D-printed in collaboration with shoe designer Rem D. Koolhaas, the founder of United Nude.

ABOVE
A dress from the *Wilderness Embodied* collection, 2013, featuring a sculpted fur texture, 3D-printed in resin composite using stereolithography

OPPOSITE
The shoes for the collection were designed by Rem D. Koolhaas of United Nude, and 3D-printed by Stratasys

LOCATION AMSTERDAM, NETHERLANDS
TECHNIQUES LASER-SINTERING, STEREOLITHOGRAPHY, HIGH-SPEED DIGITAL PHOTOGRAPHY **MATERIALS** POLYAMIDE NYLON, ACRYLIC, RESIN, VARIOUS FABRICS
WEBSITE IRISVANHERPEN.COM

ABOVE
An ornately textured corset dress from the *Wilderness Embodied* collection (left), 2013, 3D-printed in resin composite using stereolithography; the 'water dress', from the *Crystallization* collection (right), 2010, created in collaboration with Benthem Crouwel Architekten

OPPOSITE
Sculptural corset dress, from the *Escapism* collection, 2011, created in collaboration with Daniel Widrig and 3D-printed in laser-sintered polyamide nylon by Materialise

'Computer modelling and 3D-printing have, for the first time, enabled me to translate the image in my mind immediately into physical three-dimensional form. Before, I would have had a step in between, where the three-dimensional image in my mind first had to become a two-dimensional design on paper.'

'I am inspired by the struggle to achieve a "perfect" result with limited means. Although the digital domain seems to offer unlimited potential, working at this level is a big challenge.'

ERIC VAN STRAATEN

FINDING HUMAN PERFECTION IN THE LIMITS OF TECHNOLOGY

ABOVE
BambiBait, 2012,
56 × 22 × 22 cm
(22 × 9 × 9 in.)

OPPOSITE, TOP
Little Mermaid (top), 2013,
18 × 38 × 23 cm (7 × 15 × 9 in.);
Lumi (bottom), 2012,
48 × 20 × 20 cm (19 × 8 × 8 in.)

Setting out to create 'portraits' that reflect contemporary culture's fascination with adolescent youth – capturing dreams, fears and the little demons in our thoughts – sculptor Eric van Straaten takes inspiration from the youth culture of modern Japan and 1970s America, with references to Degas's *Little Dancer*, Nabokov's *Lolita* and Mary Pipher's book, *Reviving Ophelia*.

His unique, finely honed technique is a leading example of the translation of an immaculate 3D digital model into a perfect physical form. This combination of 3D-modelling and multi-colour 3D-printing requires great technical skill: although the print process may only take around twelve hours to complete, the modelling phase for each sculpture can take weeks, or even months. To achieve sculptures with a compelling level of hyper-(sur)realism – with subversive twists on kitsch, and the exquisite qualities of sugar craft – he chooses a fabrication technique that leaves no marks of the maker.

Van Straaten gradually sculpts each piece using a range of 3D-modelling and rendering software packages, transferring between platforms to achieve the desired form, colour effects and textural finishes. The final digital model is then printed through an advanced additive layering technique using multi-coloured ceramic composite powders as the medium, building up the colour gradients in ultra-high definition. The resulting ceramic sculptures do not need additional firing, as the powder is fused by laser during the printing process.

LOCATION HAARLEM, NETHERLANDS **TECHNIQUES** CAD-MODELLING, COLOUR 3D-PRINTING **MATERIALS** COMPOSITE CERAMIC POWDER **WEBSITE** ERICVANSTRAATEN.COM

ABOVE
Clockwise from top left:
Little Princess, 2013, 22.5 × 15 × 15 cm (9 × 6 × 6 in.);
Oeroeboeroe, 2011, 37 × 22 × 20 cm (15 × 9 × 8 in.);
Fallen Angel, 2011, 20 × 29 × 20 cm (8 × 11 × 8 in.);
Humming New, 2013, 22.5 × 15 × 15 cm (9 × 6 × 6 in.)

OPPOSITE
PiezaH, 2014, 115 × 45 × 35 cm (45 × 18 × 14 in.)

MICHAELLA JANSE VAN VUUREN

ADVANCING THE RELATIONSHIP BETWEEN COUTURE AND ENGINEERING

OPPOSITE
Garden of Eden collection, 2014,
3D-printed by Stratasys

Michaella Janse van Vuuren uses the most advanced digital manufacturing technologies available to create extraordinary, complex pieces that bridge the divide between art and engineering. Her most challenging project to date has been the *Garden of Eden* collection (opposite) of couture fashion pieces, which can be individually made to order – customized both in fit and colourway – using the very latest multi-material, multi-colour 3D-printing technologies.

By using the Stratasys Objet500 Connex3 printer, Van Vuuren is able to realize her designs in a revolutionary way, building up rigid structural and flexible rubber parts in the same printing process, with an almost unlimited colour palette. Illustrating the global nature of the skills involved in today's artisanal digital processes, the *Garden of Eden* collection required a virtual collaboration across three continents: digital sculpting by the designer in South Africa, followed by colour 3D-printing at Stratasys in Israel and the enabling of customization of the corset and shoes by Uformia software in Norway.

Van Vuuren previously worked with wax printing to enable the traditional metal casting of complicated forms, including her *Gold Fish* jewelry, and is now experimenting with the potential of direct metal printing, creating sculptural pieces such as the curious *Sea Dog*, which is created in one piece but with individual moving parts, using the direct metal laser-sintering process.

LOCATION FAERIE GLEN, SOUTH AFRICA **TECHNIQUES** 3D-MODELLING, 3D-PRINTING, LASER-SINTERING, WAX CASTING, DIRECT METAL LASER-SINTERING **MATERIALS** RESIN, RUBBER, 18-CARAT GOLD, BRONZE **WEBSITE** NOMILI.CO.ZA

'What I love about the process of creation is
that communication is facilitated by my drawings.
My art is used to communicate ideas fluidly between
the different disciplines of design, material
engineering and software development.'

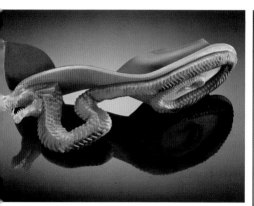

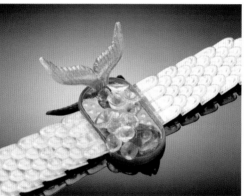

ABOVE
Serpent Shoe (top left), with low heel
and sole; and colour variations of the *Fish
Bracelet* (bottom left and right), both from
the *Garden of Eden* collection, 2014

THIS PAGE
Colour variations of the *Coral Bracelet* (left), from the *Garden of Eden* collection, 2014; *Sea Dog* (right), a sculptural piece with individual moving parts, created in one piece using the direct metal laser-sintering technique

ICON

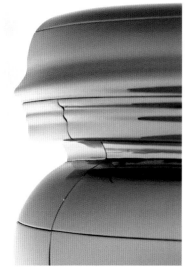

THESE PAGES
Lectori Salutem, 2010, 77 ×
242.4 × 110.7 cm (30 × 95 × 44
in.); when viewed from a certain
angle, the outline reveals the
profile of a human face (top)

JEROEN VERHOEVEN

FAIRYTALES IN CONTEMPORARY MANUFACTURING

Jeroen Verhoeven combines highly skilled material craftsmanship with complex industrial fabrication techniques to transform simple materials into extraordinary objects. For his most celebrated work, *Cinderella Table* (overleaf), he morphed together two digital sketches of the silhouettes of a seventeenth-century console and an eighteenth-century commode to create a single, three-dimensional form: a table with two contrasting personalities, depending on which side it is viewed side from.

This digital model was sliced into fifty-seven vertical pieces, each 80mm (3-in.) thick and individually cut from thin sheets of birch plywood, using CNC machines that carved the wood on five axes – challenging the abilities of the technology to its maximum – to create the unique concave and convex details of each slice. These slices were then glued together, and the whole surface smoothed and finished by hand. Versions of the table are in the permanent collections of the Victoria & Albert Museum, London, and the Museum of Modern Art, New York.

The form of a more recent work, *Lectori Salutem* (these pages), took a similar digital-modelling process, this time starting with the facial silhouettes of Jeroen's two colleagues. The surface of the model was carved into 150 panels, held in place by hundreds of internal connecting ribs; detailing the panels and ribs required a total of 700 CAD drawings. The stainless-steel panels were realized by advanced CNC machines more commonly associated with the automotive industry, and each one was laser-cut and shaped in an aluminium-pressing mould, while the ribs were laser-cut and etched with a serial number to aid assembly. The panels were assembled using 2,300 bolts, and the whole surface polished to a mirror shine.

LOCATION ROTTERDAM, NETHERLANDS **PROJECT** *CINDERELLA TABLE* (2004-7) AND *LECTORI SALUTEM* (2010) **TECHNIQUES** CAD-MODELLING, CNC CUTTING/PRESSING **MATERIALS** BIRCH PLYWOOD; STAINLESS STEEL **WEBSITE** DEMAKERSVAN.COM

258   DIGITAL HANDMADE

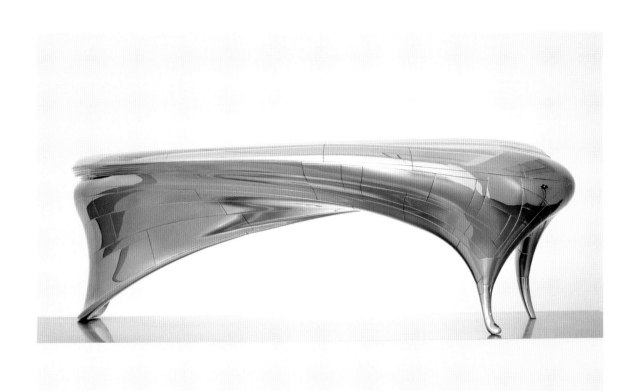

THESE PAGES
Cinderella Table, 2004–7, 80 × 131.1 × 101.6 cm (31 × 52 ×
40 in.), CNC-milled birch plywood. The outlines of the
eighteenth-century commode and the seventeenth-century
console are both visible from this angle (above); the differing
profiles of the two ends of the table meet and morph across
the surface (opposite bottom)

'I look for the path of resistance – the path
through which new things are born. These
machines made for mass production are
far more interesting if you push them to
extremes and make something unique.'

MARCEL WANDERS

SCULPTING A FROZEN MOMENT IN TIME

An early sensation in showcasing the ability of 3D-printing to produce complex, formerly 'impossible' three-dimensional shapes, this series of five vases – *Coryza*, *Influenza*, *Ozaena*, *Pollinosis* and *Sinusitis* – was inspired by five diseases of the nasal cavity that cause sneezing.

The airborne 'rain' issuing from sneezing patients suffering from these conditions was digitally captured, in flight, by a scanner equipped with a nano-lens able to scan the density of microscopic particles. One rain particle from each patient was selected, magnified 1,000 times and translated into a wire mesh digital model, which was refined and hollowed out to create the final form for each vase.

Each vase form was built using selective laser-sintering in polyamide. The designs have also been created in black polyamide, gold plating and cast bronze. Created for Cappellini, the project won *Wired* magazine's Technology Award in 2001, and the original collection of five vases has since been purchased by the Stedelijk Museum, Amsterdam.

OPPOSITE
Pollinosis, 15 × 15 × 15 cm (6 × 6 × 6 in.), from the *Airborne Snotty Vases* collection, 2001, 3D-printed and laser-sintered in polyamide nylon

LOCATION AMSTERDAM, NETHERLANDS **PROJECT** *AIRBORNE SNOTTY VASES* (2001) **TECHNIQUES** DIGITAL PHOTOGRAPHY, 3D-MODELLING, 3D-PRINTING, CASTING **MATERIALS** POLYAMIDE NYLON, GOLD, BRONZE **WEBSITE** MARCELWANDERS.COM

'I don't focus on a specific process. I like the surprising element of combining traditional crafts with innovative digital tools, which evokes new connections and impacts the design in interesting ways without overtaking the invigorating festivity, fantasy and sensuality I seek with my work.'

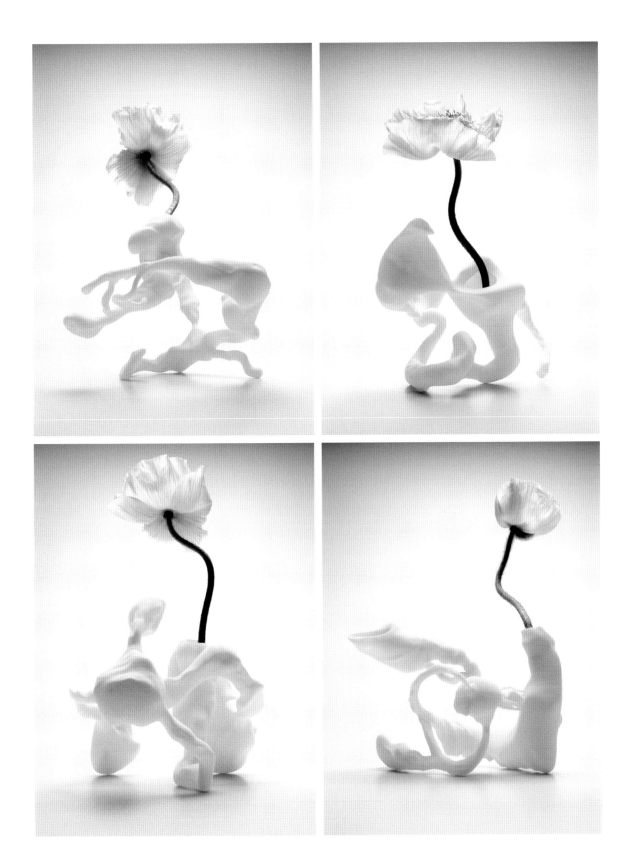

JO HAYES WARD

FREEING THE TRADITIONS OF METALSMITHING

The experimental, award-winning jewelry designs of young metalsmith Jo Hayes Ward feature distinctive pieces of precious metal, constructed from tiny building blocks and arranged in complex filigree structures that reference mathematical, scientific and organic patterns. A combination of CAD, rapid-prototyping, lost-wax casting and traditional metalworking skills are employed in the making of each piece. The design is 3D-printed in wax, creating a solid form that is then used to cast the chosen metal, and the final piece is finished by hand.

In the case of the *Hex* collection of rings, the process of rapid-prototyping in wax leaves a fine texture of lines on the surface that are transferred to the metal casting. Ward views these lines as characterful machine marks and chooses to leave them as an additional exploration of the pattern and design, rather than polishing them away. The production method she has perfected enables the creation of finely textured pieces that would be incredibly challenging, time-consuming and costly to realize by hand – particularly when it comes to the precision required in forming the tiny corner details of the stacking *Hex* rings.

ABOVE
Antique Sphere Ring, 2009, oxidized silver

OPPOSITE
Cushion Ring, 2011, 18-carat yellow gold

LOCATION LONDON, UK **TECHNIQUES** CAD-MODELLING, 3D WAX-PRINTING, LOST-WAX CASTING, TRADITIONAL METALWORKING **MATERIALS** PRECIOUS METALS **WEBSITE** JOHAYES.COM

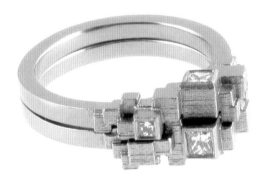

ABOVE
Hex stacking rings (top left and right), in 18-carat yellow gold,
18-carat warm-white gold, 18-carat white gold and palladium;
and *Large Stack Ring* (bottom left), 2011, in 18-carat warm-
white gold and cold-white gold

OPPOSITE
Random Oval Necklace (top), 2008, in silver, stainless steel
and aluminium; and *Convex Hex* and *Ripple Hex* brooches
(bottom), 2012, in oxidized silver and silver

'I do need to work within the boundaries of how finely I can actually print and cast something, and still consider the wearability and weight of a piece. But ultimately there is a huge amount that can be explored with this technology.'

'Both traditional and digital tools encourage us to experiment. Digital tools, especially in combination with 3D-printing, become very powerful, because almost anything in your imagination can be built. They become an important inspirational part of the design process.'

WERTELOBERFELL

THE TACTILITY OF FRACTAL MATHEMATICAL STRUCTURES

OPPOSITE, TOP
Entity lighting collection, 2014, 3D-printed in sintered polyamide nylon, produced with the Philips Hue lighting system

OPPOSITE, BOTTOM
Fractal Table, 2007, designed in collaboration with Matthias Bär and produced with Materialise.MGX

Gernot Oberfell and Jan Wertel view digital technologies and new manufacturing processes as sources for inspiration and experimentation, combining them with the logic and beauty of organic structures. Their *Fractal Table* design derives from studies of the fractal growth patterns seen in natural forms. Created using simulation software, the tree-like forms of the construction are generated through multiple branching stems, each time reducing in dimension, as described by mathematical algorithms. The structure begins with unorganized trunks at floor level, and becomes progressively more organized until it ends in a regular flat grid of the smallest twigs.

Conceived in collaboration with designer Matthias Bär, the form of the table would be impossible to manufacture without rapid-prototyping technology. Both in terms of size and complexity, the table pushes the manufacturing process to its limits. It is fabricated as a single piece, in epoxy resin, using the process of stereolithography. *Fractal Table* was created in partnership with the pioneering 3D-printing production studio Materialise, and is now in the permanent collections of the Metropolitan Museum of Art, New York; the Victoria & Albert Museum, London; and the Montreal Museum of Fine Arts.

LOCATION BERLIN, GERMANY **TECHNIQUES** CAD-MODELLING, STEREOLITHOGRAPHY **MATERIALS** EPOXY RESIN
WEBSITE WERTELOBERFELL.COM

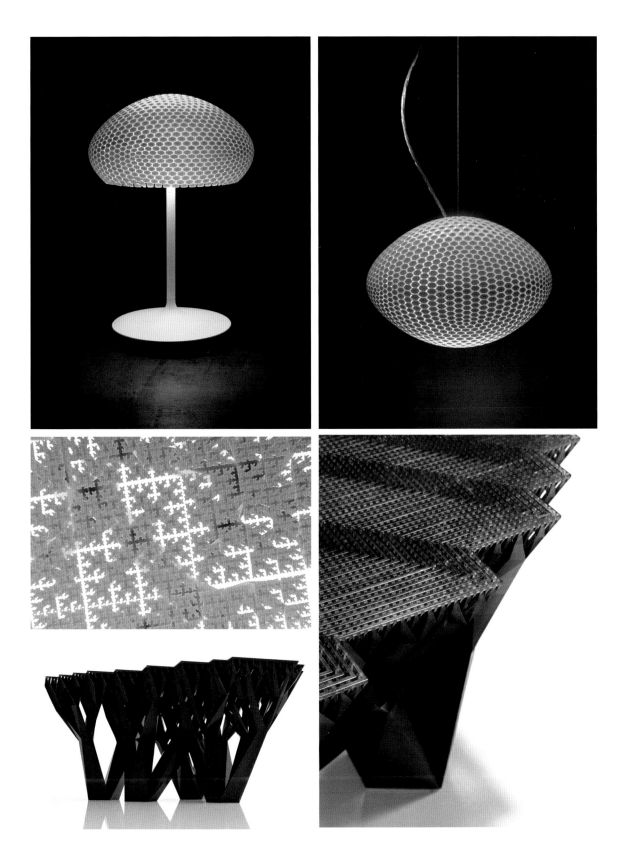

'I am fascinated by the meeting point of Eastern values, future technology and the potential to be found in combining a variety of disciplines to create something that is a constant progression. For me, good design is inspired by the process.'

ZHANG ZHOUJIE

AN AESTHETIC BORN OF THE DIGITAL GENERATION

ABOVE
Object # SQN3-A, 2011, one of many chair designs produced by the *Endless Forms* software

OPPOSITE
A chair from the *Brass* collection, 2011–ongoing, the first series developed with *Endless Forms*

Industrial designer Zhang Zhoujie blends Chinese fine-art values with Western design methodology, digital engineering and handcraftsmanship in the making of each of his furniture designs. His most recognized project to date is the *Endless Forms* series, which uses a proprietary 'digitized fabrication system' that produces personalized chairs designed to exactly fit an individual's seated pose. (The system is still being developed; the chairs shown here are based on Zhoujie's measurements, gathered using the proposed process.)

The process begins by measuring the way in which a person sits on a test chair. The imprint left by the individual's shape in the soft surface covering the seat and back is 3D-scanned, resulting in a digital model of the dimensions and pressure points associated with each person. The data is then refined to create a unique three-dimensional mesh of precise triangular facets, of varying sizes and dimensions. This digital mesh is flattened into a two-dimensional pattern that is used as the template for a laser-cutting machine, which slices the triangles out of sheets of stainless steel, titanium or brass.

The triangles are then folded by hand to create precise angles, before the pieces are glued and secured into place with fibreglass. Each chair is constructed in two halves, and then welded together down the centre for strength and polished to finish. Further furniture items are being developed, all generated utilizing the same process of physical model through fractal evolution.

LOCATION SHANGHAI, CHINA **TECHNIQUES** 3D-SCANNING, LASER-CUTTING, HAND-ASSEMBLY AND FINISHING **MATERIALS** STAINLESS STEEL, TITANIUM, BRASS **WEBSITE** ZHANGZHOUJIE.COM

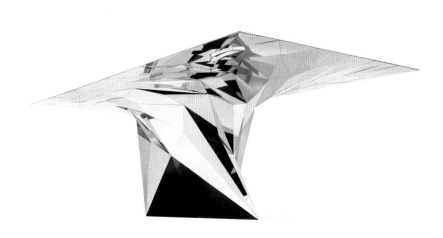

ABOVE
Digital Tornado, 2013, tables, stainless steel (top)
and brass (bottom)

OPPOSITE
Clockwise from top:
Object #SQN5-T table, 2011; *Object # SQN1-M*
public bench, 2012; *Object # ET2-B9* stool, 2011,
all in stainless-steel

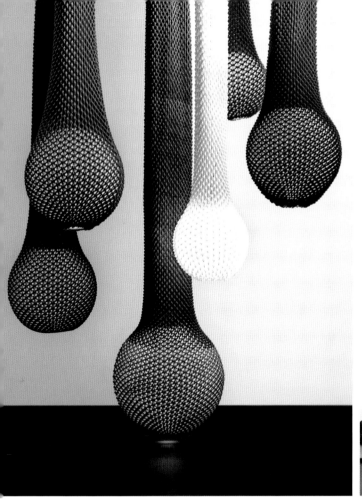

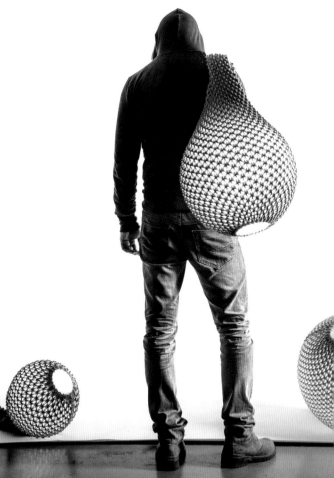

'My working method
continuously switches between
material and digital tools. The
relationship between them leads
to original results that introduce
a new, third element – not
defined as the product of either
one or the other.'

Industrial designer Ariel Zuckerman combines digital and traditional manufacturing processes to bring a sharp clarity to the form, structure and texture of his work. Alongside his commercial product designs, his individual creations have appeared in museums and galleries worldwide.

The *Knitted* collection of lamps (above), created in collaboration with Oded Sapir, contrasts the sleek silhouette of a translucent sphere with the warm texture of a knitted skin. The pattern for this acrylic knitted skin was designed digitally, together with textile designer Adva Bruner, to incorporate a delicate three-dimensional structure of peaks and openings, ensuring a robust surface with large light penetration.

The feathered lattice design is produced as a seamless tube by a knitting machine, resulting in an immaculate execution of the pattern. Each tube is finished by a dressmaker with wire and a contrasting woollen crochet stitch, and stretched over an acrylic sphere, made from a translucent material using conventional rotational moulding.

The *Folded* series (overleaf) applies paper-craft techniques such as scoring, folding, stretching and twisting to thin sheets of walnut and oak veneer. Each lampshade is made from a single sheet; the outline is laser-cut and the surface is gently laser-etched with a design of geometric lines. The lampshades are then finished by hand, using the pattern of scored lines to fold and sculpt each final shape with precision.

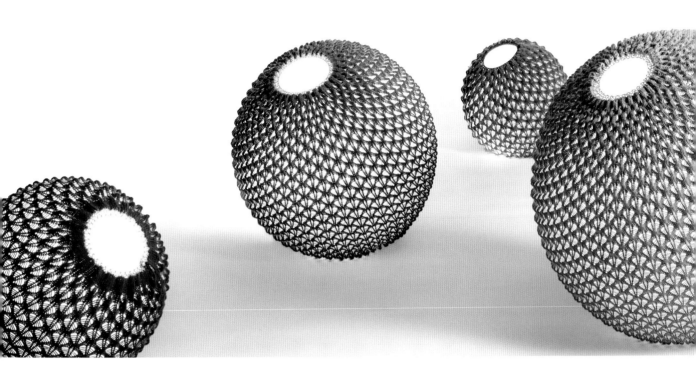

ARIEL ZUCKERMAN

CRAFTING THE WARMING
TEXTURE OF LIGHT

LOCATION TEL AVIV, ISRAEL **TECHNIQUES** CAD-MODELLING,
DIGITAL KNITTING, ROTATIONAL MOULDING, LASER-ETCHING
MATERIALS ACRYLIC, ACRYLIC THREADS, WOOD VENEERS
WEBSITE ARIEL-DESIGN.COM

THESE PAGES
Folded collection, 2014, floor, ceiling and desk
lamps, made from single sheets of oak and
walnut veneer

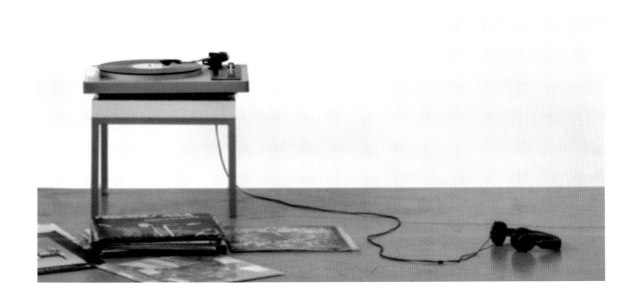

BIOGRAPHIES

JEKATERINA APALE

Born and now based in Riga, Latvia, Jekaterina Apale specialized in textiles at the Art Academy of Latvia. She took part in an Erasmus Programme, studying textiles at the University of Berlin, and participated in the Nord Balt Textile Art project, in Norway, which introduced her to the potential of the TC1 digital loom. She went on to teach weaving at the Art Academy of Latvia, using the TC1 loom, the first of its kind in the country. Her work has been exhibited worldwide.

ASSA ASHUACH

Israeli-born, London-based designer Assa Ashuach challenges and redefines the form and function of everyday products at his studio, assisted by a network of experts across the design, science and manufacturing sectors. He founded Digital Forming, a software house that introduced the concept of 'user co-design' as a new industrial design method. In 2009, he participated in the *Future of Manufacturing* exhibition, celebrating the 100th anniversary of the Science Museum, London. Ashuach is a research fellow and course leader at the Cass Faculty of Art, Architecture and Design, London.

ATMOS

Artist and architect Alex Haw directs Atmos, an award-winning multi-disciplinary studio, which produces complex, multi-sensorial work from small-scale product-design to large-scale masterplans. Haw graduated with a Fulbright grant from Princeton University, and a First from the Bartlett School of Architecture, University College London. He has taught design studios at the Architectural Association, Cambridge University, the Royal College of Art and the Vienna University of Technology, and runs regular crowd-sourced explorations of world food.

JORGE AYALA

Born in Mexico City, and now living and working in Paris, designer Jorge Ayala founded [Ay]A in 2011 as a global design laboratory, committed to cutting-edge research and material experimentation. Through computational tactics and physical innovation, Ayala tailors architecture to different disciplines: art, chemistry, landscape urbanism, engineering, marketing, music and editorial, as well as product and clothing design. In 2012 Ayala expanded his entrepreneurial ambition into 'digital couture' fashion.

BARRY X BALL

Artist Barry X Ball employs a complex array of advanced technology and artisanal methods, to realize his *Portrait*, *Masterpiece* and *Scholars' Rock* series in exotic stones. His work has been exhibited, collected and received critical attention worldwide. He is represented by Sperone Westwater Gallery, New York; Galerie Nathalie Obadia, Paris; Long March Space, Beijing; McCabe Fine Art, Stockholm; ConnerSmith, Washington, DC; Galleria Michela Rizzo, Venice; 100 Tonson Gallery, Bangkok; and the Louise Alexander Gallery, Sardinia. Ball is based in New York.

LOUISE LEMIEUX BÉRUBÉ

A graduate of the Université du Québec, Louise Lemieux Bérubé combines refined skills in photography, computerized composition and Jacquard weaving in her work. Her creations have been exhibited internationally and are in private and public collections around the world, including the Canadian Embassy, London; German Museum of Technology, Berlin; and Place des Arts, Montreal. She is the co-founder of the Montreal Centre for Contemporary Textiles, the author of *Le tissage créateur* and co-author of *Unwinding the Threads*.

FRANCIS BITONTI

Designer Francis Bitonti is ushering in a new manufacturing paradigm through his blend of computational design techniques and emerging manufacturing technologies. He sees computer methodologies, smart materials and interactive environments as opportunities to create new aesthetic languages for our built environment. His work has been published internationally, and exhibited at the Museum of Arts and Design and the Cooper-Hewitt National Design Museum, both in New York. He lives and works in New York.

ISAÏE BLOCH

Belgian architect Isaïe Bloch is the founder of Eragatory, a creative studio with a focus on design for digital fabrication. After receiving his first MA in Experimental Architecture from Sint-Lucas Architectuur, Ghent, he joined the Excessive postgraduate programme in 2010, led by Hernan Diaz Alonso, at Die Angewandte, Vienna, for his second. Bloch's ongoing research and design work are focused on the correlation between craftsmanship and additive manufacturing across domains that include architecture, fashion and plastic arts.

TORD BOONTJE

Tord Boontje set up his eponymous studio in 1996, in London. Educated at Eindhoven Design Academy and the Royal College of Art, he returned to the RCA in 2009 as Professor and Head of Design Products, a position he held for four years. Boontje's designs are in the permanent collections of the Victoria & Albert Museum and Tate Modern, both in London, and the Museum of Modern Art, New York, among others, and his iconic *Garland Light* design for Habitat can be found in over half a million homes worldwide.

VALISSA BUTTERWORTH

Ceramicist Valissa Butterworth obtained a Diploma of Arts from the Holmesglen Institute, Melbourne, and was a Fine Art Graduate, specializing in ceramics, at RMIT, Melbourne. She is now recognized through multiple awards and exhibitions in her native Australia. Her working process is notable for its experimental, open approach to combining cutting-edge and traditional craft skills in the making of her tableware and lighting designs, all of which are available through her own studio, The Mod Collective.

EMILY COBB

US-based jewelry designer Emily Cobb received her MFA in Metals/Jewelry/CAD-CAM from Tyler School of Art, Temple University, in Philadelphia. She is currently teaching at the University of the Arts, Philadelphia, and Towson University, in Maryland. Her experimental use of emerging fabrication technologies and non-traditional materials in the creation of her illustrative, fairy-tale pieces has gained her recognition and acclaim. Her work has been published internationally, and exhibited at the Delaware Center for the Contemporary Arts.

LIA COOK

Textile artist Lia Cook works in a variety of media, combining photography, weaving, painting and digital technology. Working together with neuroscientists, she explores the nature of the emotional response to the tactile quality of woven faces. She has exhibited her work internationally, most recently in Liege, Belgium; Chicago, Illinois; and Hangzhou, China. Her works are in the permanent collections of the Metropolitan Museum of Art, New York; Smithsonian Museum, Washington, DC; National Gallery of Australia; and the National Silk Museum, China, among others. She is based in Berkeley, California.

ELENA CORCHERO

Award-winning designer Elena Corchero envisions a future where technology helps us become more human and less machine-led. Born in Lanzarote, Spain, and now living and working in London, Corchero gained a Licenciatura in Fine Arts from the University of La Laguna, Spain, specialized in digital arts in Germany, and gained an MA in Textile Futures from Central Saint Martins, London. She was a research associate in the Human Connectedness group at MIT Media Lab Europe, and is an expert on smart materials and wearable technologies, with a focus on sustainability.

MICHIEL CORNELISSEN

Michiel Cornelissen combines a background in industrial design with an exploration into the possibilities of digital fabrication and the mass-customization of products. He studied design engineering at the Delft University of Technology, before working at Phillips Design for over a decade. His design studio, Michiel Cornelissen Ontwerp, combines work for clients with the creation of his own products range, including jewelry, homeware and electronics accessories. His work is widely available to purchase, and receives much attention in the design press.

LIONEL T. DEAN

Lionel T. Dean is Reader in Digital Arts in the School of Design, De Montfort University, Leicester, where he heads a research group on digital design and manufacturing technologies. His work is at the forefront of digital-making, exploring the traditional definitions of art, craft and design practice, and his groundbreaking designs have received international acclaim. In 2003 he founded FutureFactories, a studio focused exclusively on 3D-printing technologies and developing computational design methodologies.

WIM DELVOYE

Wim Delvoye is a Belgian neo-conceptual artist known for his inventive, often controversial projects. He has an eclectic oeuvre, covering a range of themes, from bodily functions to the Catholic church and the seventeenth-century Flemish Baroque, while embracing digital-fabrication technologies in the production of his intricate and large-scale metalworks. He lives and works in Ghent; prior to that he ran an 'Art Farm' in Shanghai until a court judged his pig-tattoo projects to be illegal.

OLAF DIEGEL

Olaf Diegel is a longstanding educator and practitioner of engineering design, with a passion for 3D-printing and other advanced manufacturing technologies. His radical, award-winning ODD brand of 3D-printed electric guitars is featured in the mobile National Guitar Museum in the US. A New Zealander, Diegel is Professor of Product Development in the Faculty of Engineering, Lund University, Sweden. His guitars are available from the 3D-printing platform Cubify.

DAVID D'IMPERIO

David D'Imperio's work straddles the border between the organic world and the mechanical one, where geometry and mathematical order meet the abstract and random. He encourages people to look at his lighting not as design objects, with the sole purpose of producing light, but as sculpture. His background as a graphic designer and draughtsman is evident in his old-school way of working, drawing all of his designs on paper before employing digital technology for precision alignment in production.

MICHAEL EDEN

Already a well-respected and established potter, Michael Eden completed an MPhil at the Royal College of Art, London, in 2008. Utilizing and developing a combination of drawing, 3D software, traditional hand-skills and digital technology, his research brings together revolutionary tools and materials – with his *Wedgwoodn't Tureen*, to worldwide acclaim. Since then, Eden has continued to push digital technology further, producing ever-more complex and larger works that retain a unique quality and aesthetic. He is represented by Adrian Sassoon, London.

FACTUM ARTE

Founded by Adam Lowe, the Factum Arte studio, based in Madrid, Spain, consists of a team of artists, technicians and conservators dedicated to digital mediation, both in the production of works for contemporary artists and of facsimiles as part of a coherent approach to preservation, monitoring and dissemination. Working across a number of large-scale projects, the workshop has gained a reputation for the uncompromising nature of its work and an obsessive commitment to pushing the boundaries separating technology and art.

FRONT

The works of Swedish design group Front – Sofia Lagerkvist, Charlotte von der Lancken and Anna Lindgren – are based on common discussions, explorations and experiments. All three members of the team are involved in projects from initial idea to final product. Their designs often communicate a story to the observer about the design process, the material it is made from or conventions within the design field. Fascinated by magic, the Front team assigns part of the making process to animals, computers or machines.

ADAM NATHANIEL FURMAN

Adam Nathaniel Furman is a London-based designer, writer and artist. He graduated with honours from the Architectural Association, has worked with OMA and Ron Arad, and has taught at the AA Cardiff, Sint-Lucas Architectuur, Ghent, and Tel Aviv University. Furman is a columnist for the *RIBA Journal* and *The Architectural Review*, and creates a wide range of design projects, from *Identity Parade*, exhibited at the Design Museum, London, to 3D-printed ceramics, architectural projects and poetry.

BRAM GEENEN

Bram Geenen established his design studio in 2008 upon graduating from Utrecht School of the Arts. His early work focused on the use of 3D-printing to create super-lightweight furniture. His *Gaudí Stool* and *Gaudí Chair* received international acclaim, and were acquired by the Design Museum, Barcelona. In 2011, the Aram Gallery, London, featured an overview of his early work. His current project, Wevolver.com, is a website for exploring, sharing and creating open-source technology, including robotics and 3D-printers.

ANTONY GORMLEY

Turner prize-winning artist Antony Gormley OBE has had many solo shows – at the Centro Cultural Banco do Brasil; Deichtorhallen, Hamburg; Hermitage Museum, St Petersburg; Kunsthaus Bregenz; Hayward Gallery, London; Kunsthalle zu Kiel; Malmö Konsthall; and the Louisiana Museum of Modern Art, in Humlebæk, Denmark – and participated in group shows at the Venice Biennale and Documenta 8, in Kassel Germany. Major public works include *Angel of the North* and *Another Place*, both in the UK, and *Exposure*, in the Netherlands. He is a member of the Royal Academy and is a Trustee of the British Museum.

DAVID GRAAS

Dutch designer David Graas studied Product Design at the Gerrit Rietveld Academie, Amsterdam. Since 2004 he has worked as an independent product designer, investigating the relationship between functional objects and their users, how these objects are valued and why. Not caring for 'pretty things', his focus lies with ideas, rather than style, prolonging the lifespan of products in an era where the cycle of fashion spins ever faster. His work has been showcased in exhibitions in Paris, New York, Osaka and Moscow.

BATHSHEBA GROSSMAN

Artist and designer Bathsheba Grossman specializes in complex three-dimensional computer-modelling techniques for 3D-printing. She studied mathematics at Yale University, followed by sculpture at the University of Pennsylvania, while working during the day as a programmer. Over the following two decades, as software and fabrication technologies developed, Grossman found an influential niche as an artist and retailer of 3D-printed products, and has become an expert voice on the 3D-printing revolution.

GT2P

GT2P (Great Things To People) is a creative studio, based in Santiago, Chile, which is involved in projects across architecture, art and design. The team describes a continuous process of research and experimentation in digital crafting, promoting new encounters between technologies and the richness of their locality expressed in traditional materials and techniques. GT2P exhibits globally, and in 2014 initiated the project *Losing My America* to promote disappearing traditional crafts and to build bridges between craft culture and the commercial, digitized world.

MICHAEL HANSMEYER

Michael Hansmeyer is a Swiss architect and programmer who explores the use of algorithms and computation to generate architectural form. Recent projects include the installation *Sixth Order* at the Gwangju Design Biennale, and a 3D-printed grotto for the 2013 FRAC Archilab exhibition. Previously based in the CAAD group at ETH Zurich, he is currently visiting architecture professor at Southeast University, Nanjing. Hansmeyer holds an M.Arch from Columbia University and an MBA from INSEAD Fontainebleau.

JOSHUA HARKER

Chicago-based artist Joshua Harker is a pioneer in the medium of 3D-printing, exploring new possibilities in design and manufacturing. Known for his large-scale projection mapped installation sculptures, his exploration and use of digital mediums has brought him international recognition, and his work has been published worldwide. Harker's sculpture *Crania Anatomica Filigre: Me to You* is the third most-funded arts project in the history of the Kickstarter crowd-funding website.

DEL HARROW

Del Harrow is Associate Professor at Colorado State University, where he teaches sculpture, digital fabrication and ceramics. He has lectured at Pennsylvania State University and the Harvard University Graduate School of Design, and has exhibited at the Milwaukee Art Museum; Denver Art Museum; Vox Populi, Philadelphia; and the Harvey Meadows Gallery, Aspen, Colorado. He is represented by Haw Contemporary, Kansas City.

PATRICK HOET

Belgian optician Patrick Hoet's family connections in the industry go back to 1884. Originally the creative mind behind eyewear company Theo, Hoet now develops and distributes under his own name. The company, which launched the first high-end 3D-printed eyewear in titanium, is a small family business, to be taken over eventually by his three daughters: Bieke, Lieselotte and Jozefien.

RALF HOLLEIS

Award-winning industrial designer Ralf Holleis had just graduated from Coburg University of Applied Sciences, Bavaria, when he created the bespoke fixed-gear, track bike brand VORWaeRTZ. The design immediately garnered international press attention for his refined use of 3D-printing, combined with traditional bike-making craftsmanship, offering a personalized and highly accurate production process.

MONIKA HORCICOVÁ

Sculptural artist Monika Horcicová graduated from the Faculty of Fine Arts, Brno University of Technology, where she studied under the tutelage of Michal Gabriel and Tomáš Medek. Her work, which focuses on changing perceptions of the human body after death, has been exhibited in galleries in the Czech Republic, Switzerland, Paris, London and New York.

ANTHONY HORRIGAN

The work of ceramics designer Anthony Horrigan has been recognized with a Future Makers award for innovation from the Crafts Council of Ireland. Since graduating with an MA in Ceramic Design from Staffordshire University, Horrigan has designed for some of the leading ceramic manufacturers in the UK and Ireland, including Wedgwood, Aynsley China, Flux Stoke on Trent and Marks & Spencer. He is currently an in-house designer for Belleek Pottery in Northern Ireland.

DORRY HSU

Experimental jewelry and accessories designer Dorry Hsu is originally from Taipei, and now resides in London. She studied at the Royal College of Art, which she cites as a key turning point in her career and influential in her vision as an artist. She has received a number of talent-support awards, and her jewelry designs have been featured at the 3D Printshow in London, Paris and New York; Goldsmiths, University of London; the Victoria & Albert Museum; and Art Revolution Taipei. Her work is sold as far afield as Poland and Shanghai.

INFLEXIONS

Inflexions, based in Bagnolet, France, was founded by François Brument and Sonia Laugier, two designers with a shared interest in digital conception, fabrication and distribution processes. Brument teaches at the École Supérieure d'Art et Design de Saint-Etienne, specializing in programming design and industrial production, while Laugier is an engineer and designer, graduating from the École Centrale de Nantes. In 2014 they were artists-in-residence at the Taiwan Ceramics Biennale, where they collaborated with local artists and devised new digital-production techniques for ceramics.

AKI INOMATA

Japanese artist and designer Aki Inomata graduated with an MFA in Inter-Media Art from Tokyo University of the Arts. She has staged solo shows in Japan, China and the US, and her work has been exhibited in New York, Paris and London. Her intricate, crafted approach to working with digital modelling and fabrication technologies, with a focus on adaptation, protection and integrating work with living creatures and natural processes, has gained her recognition in the international press.

LINLIN & PIERRE-YVES JACQUES

Linlin and Pierre-Yves Jacques are artists in the fields of digital creation and visual 3D-production. Their pioneering organic sculptures are realized through a joint creative process, fusing their Chinese and French backgrounds, and demonstrate what is possible in the medium of 3D-printing for sculpture. Their work has been been exhibited in Kuala Lumpur, New York, Tokyo, Hong Kong, London and Paris.

SOPHIE KAHN

Sculptor Sophie Kahn earned a BA (Hons) in Fine Art and History of Art at Goldsmiths, University of London, and an MFA in Art and Technology Studies at the School of the Art Institute of Chicago. She has taught at Columbia College Chicago, and the Pratt Institute, Brooklyn, and has exhibited in Los Angeles, London, Sydney, Tokyo, Osaka and Seoul. In 2011, Kahn was named Digital and Electronic Arts Fellow, New York Foundation for the Arts.

JORIS LAARMAN

A graduate of the Design Academy Eindhoven, Joris Laarman first gained notoriety with his rococo radiator *Heatwave*, later picked up by Droog. He has taught at the Architectural Association and the Gerrit Rietveld Academie, Amsterdam, and his designs are in the collections of the Victoria & Albert Museum, London, and the Museum of Modern Art, New York. In 2004, he founded an experimental design lab with film-maker Anita Star.

CINNAMON LEE

Artist and designer Cinnamon Lee specializes in the combined use of CAD, additive fabrication and traditional gold and silversmithing techniques. She has exhibited internationally and received numerous awards, and examples of her highly collectible jewelry and lighting designs can be found in the collections of the National Gallery of Australia and the Art Gallery of Western Australia.

LEE ALLEN EYEWEAR

Lee Allen Kuczewski is an optician and eyewear designer based in Rhode Island and Brooklyn, New York. With over ten years' experience in the industry, he creates bespoke eyewear for international clients. He co-founded Lee Allen Eyewear with artist Declan Halpin, who brings an expert understanding of the emerging opportunities of digital technologies in bespoke product development.

PAUL LOEBACH

Furniture and product designer Paul Loebach has a background in traditional woodworking, handed down through generations of craftsmen. He applies his hands-on design philosophy to a range of industrially manufactured objects, from furniture to lighting. His designs focus on the emotive meaning of objects, stemming from a belief that each one represents an opportunity to invoke change.

AMY ROPER LYONS

US-based jeweller Amy Roper Lyons produces bold compositions that draw from a broad palette of techniques across enamelling and metalworking. Her award-winning work has been published widely and featured in museum exhibitions and craft shows. Lyons received her BFA from the University of the Arts, Philadelphia, and has taught jewelry and enamelling at the Visual Arts Center of New Jersey and the Newark Museum, New Jersey.

LUCAS MAASSEN

Lucas Maassen began his career by designing such non-functional items as the *Nano* chair, which is so small it can only be seen through an electron microscope. Believing that in the post-digital era creating 'tools to design with' will become more important than the actual object, Maassen is developing a tool that can turn thoughts into designs. A recent project was to turn his parents' DNA into a chandelier.

MAGNOLIA EDITIONS

Artist and master printmaker Donald Farnsworth is recognized as an innovator in digital technology and weaving techniques. In 1981 he founded Magnolia Editions in Oakland, California, as a fine-art publishing company and collaborative studio. Techniques developed by the studio have revived and expanded the possibilities of processes such as photogravure and tapestry for artists including Chuck Close, Hung Liu, Kiki Smith and Masami Teraoka.

GEOFFREY MANN

Artist, designer and craftsman Geoffrey Mann heads a multi-disciplinary studio that focuses on everyday objects to form the aesthetic of its designs. His investigations into rendering the intangible encapsulates the beauty that exists apart from the material world, and he embraces collaborations within both the artisan community and commercial industry. Mann's work is exhibited internationally.

LUC MERX

Dutch native Luc Merx is interested in the borders between architecture, design and art. In the project *Rococo Relevance*, he examined the parallels between Baroque and contemporary design. His work has been published widely and exhibited at the Victoria & Albert Museum, London, and the Weißenhofgalerie, Stuttgart. Merx is currently Professor at Kaiserslautern University of Technology.

GARETH NEAL

Having established his furniture-design practice in 2002 and now working as a researcher at the University of Brighton, Gareth Neal combines the technical modes of 3D-manufacturing with the intricacy of professional craftsmanship. His work has been exhibited at the Museum of Arts and Design, New York, and the Design Museum Holon, Israel, and his *Three Draw George* chest of drawers is now part of the Victoria & Albert Museum's permanent collection.

NENDO

Pioneering design studio Nendo, founded by Oki Sato in 2002, promotes traditional craft principles alongside cutting-edge technology. The Tokyo-based studio has created many award-winning projects in architecture, product design and furniture, and their products are in the permanent collections of the Museum of Modern Art, New York; the Centre Pompidou, Paris; and the Design Museum Holon, Israel.

NERVOUS SYSTEM

Jessica Rosenkrantz and Jesse Louis Rosenberg founded Nervous System in 2007. Rosenkrantz graduated from MIT in architecture and biology, later studying at the Harvard Graduate School of Design; Rosenberg also attended MIT, majoring in mathematics. The duo's designs have been published in *Wired*, *Metropolis* and *Forbes*, and they have spoken about their generative-design process at MIT, Carnegie Mellon University and SIGGRAPH.

MARC NEWSON

Australian-born, London-based Marc Newson is one of the most successful designers of his generation. He was included in *Time* magazine's 100 Most Influential People in the World, and his work is included in the permanent collections of museums around the world. Having set records at auction, his creative output now accounts for almost 25 per cent of the contemporary-design market.

ELAINE YAN LING NG

'Techno fairy' and multimedia artist Elaine Yan Ling Ng received her MA in Textile Futures from Central Saint Martins, London, has worked with the likes of Nissan and Nokia, and been the recipient of numerous design awards, including a TED fellowship. She is founder of The Fabrick Lab, and her work has been exhibited at the Science Museum, London, and Wuhao, Beijing.

NERI OXMAN

Pioneering designer Neri Oxman is the Sony Corporation Career Development Professor of Media Arts and Sciences at the MIT Media Lab, where she founded and directs the Mediated Matter research group. She was among *Icon*'s twenty most influential architects to shape our future, and one of Fast Company's '100 most creative people'.

JAN PLECHÁC

Jan Plechác and partner Henry Wielgus met while studying at the Academy of Arts, Architecture and Design, Prague. Plechác exhibited his thesis work at Salone Satellite 2011, and has won numerous awards, including Discovery of the Year at the Czech Grand Design Awards. In 2012 the duo founded Jan Plechác & Henry Wielgus, a studio that produces work for Rossana Orlandi, Mint, Luminaire and Cappellini, among others.

MATTHEW PLUMMER-FERNANDEZ

In his work, artist and designer Matthew Plummer-Fernandez examines new sociocultural entanglements with emerging technologies. With qualifications in product and graphic design and computer-aided mechanical engineering, his interests span bots, algorithms, automation, copyright and file-sharing. He is author of the Algopop blog, and in 2014 won a Prix Ars Electronica Award of Distinction. Plummer-Fernandez is research associate and technologist at the Interaction Research Studio, Goldsmiths, University of London.

LOUIS PRATT

Louis Pratt studied sculpture at the Australian National University School of Art, and received a research scholarship from the College of Fine Arts, University of New South Wales, where he now teaches. His work is held in numerous private collections, and awards include the Mt Buller Sculpture Award and the Woollahra Small Sculpture Prize.

KARINA NØKLEBY PRESTTUN

A graduate of the Bergen National Academy of the Arts, Karina Nøkleby Presttun has a background in graphic design and creative writing. Her textiles are in the permanent collections of Kode 1, Bergen; Nordenfjeldske Kunstindustrimuseum, Trondheim; and the National Museum of Art, Architecture and Design, Oslo. Her work has also been included in exhibitions in Norway, Latvia, Lithuania and Thailand.

ANASTASIA RADEVICH

Footwear designer Anastasia Radevich lives and works in Montreal, Canada. She graduated with distinction from the London College of Fashion, followed by stints at Alexander McQueen, Nicholas Kirkwood and Bolongaro Trevor. Defining herself as not just a footwear designer, but also an artist, her work has been exhibited in Germany, Italy Canada and the US.

CÉDRIC RAGOT

Designer Cédric Ragot's creations have won a string of honours, including a Good Design Award, *Wallpaper** Design Award and two Reddot Design Awards. In 2014, he received the Best Design FiFi Award for the perfume bottle for Invictus by Paco Rabanne, and started a jewelry collection with Galerie MiniMasterpiece, in Paris. His work is in the collection of the Fonds national d'art contemporain, France.

ZACH RAVEN

After gaining a BFA from Kendall College of Art and Design, Michigan, industrial designer Zach Raven honed his skills at industrial design studios across the furniture, fashion, sports, transportation, marine and electronics sectors. His work has been exhibited in Dubai, Chicago and New York, and recognized with awards including numerous Gold and Silver NeoCon awards and NeoCon Best in Show. His boutique watch brand RVNDSGN was established in the US in 2011.

GUTO REQUENA

São Paulo-based Guto Requena was a researcher at the Center for Interactive Living Studies, University of São Paulo, for nine years, before founding Estudio Guto Requena, as well as Professor at the Panamericana School of Arts and Design and Istituto Europeo di Design. He has won many awards, lectured and exhibited internationally, hosted TV shows, and writes regularly for the press.

NADIA-ANNE RICKETTS

Having graduated in Textile Design from Central Saint Martins, London, Nadia-Anne Ricketts combines her passion for music and weaving skills with an eye for trends and developments in digital technologies. Work from her BeatWoven project has been shown at the Victoria & Albert Museum, London, and she has worked on research projects with The Centre for Digital Music, Queen Mary, University of London, in conjunction with Creativeworks London. Other collaborations include Harrods and Decorex International 2014.

ARIEL ROJO

Ariel Rojo first started designing at the age of seventeen, developing printed circuits for his grandfather's factory. He studied at the Universidad Nacional Autónoma de México, and was part of the winning team that remodelled the Zócalo of Mexico City, the third biggest plaza in the world. Rojo received special mention for designing the urban furniture. Today, Ariel Rojo Design Studio is an international firm with customers in Mexico, Europe, the USA and the Middle East. His work has been recognized in competitions, publications and exhibitions across the world.

JACK ROW

An award-winning British gold- and silversmith, Jack Row designs elegant writing instruments and accessories, intended for a discerning clientele. Working in silver, gold and platinum and incorporating precious gemstones, Row fuses traditional goldsmithing skills with the latest technology. He is a graduate of the School of Jewellery, Birmingham Institute of Art and Design, and is a Queen Elizabeth Scholarship Trust scholar Balvenie Master of Craft. His designs are available at Harrods and the Burlington Arcade, London.

LIN STANIONIS

Currently Professor of Jewelry/Metals at the University of Kansas, Lin Stanionis's creative output encompasses both jewelry and hollow-ware. Her work has been published extensively and has been shown in more than 150 national and international exhibitions. It is included in the permanent collection of Indiana University Fine Art Museum, and numerous private collections. She has received a MAA-NEA Individual Artist Fellowship, and two Creative Work Fellowships and twelve Research Awards from the University of Kansas.

ELISA STROZYK

Elisa Strozyk studied Textile and Surface Design at the Kunsthochschule in Berlin, and completed an MA in Textile Futures at Central Saint Martins, London. Her work pushes the boundaries between two and three dimensions, hard and soft materials, meanings and categories. For her experimental designs, Strozyk has received the German Design Award and the Satellite Award from the Salone del Mobile, Milan. Her work has been exhibited at Design Miami and Internationale Möbelmesse, Cologne.

LASZLO TOMPA

Laszlo Tompa is a ceramist, tile designer and wood craftsman, currently living and working in Hungary. He studied at the Moholy-Nagy University of Art and Design, Budapest, and has won many awards and fellowships. His work has been exhibited many times in Japan, and he has had solo and group shows in the UK, Austria and Spain. His innovative woodworking pieces – embracing digital technologies while staying true to the soul of the craft – have been the focus of much design press worldwide.

UNFOLD

Belgian design studio Unfold is an experimental creative platform that embraces developments in digital technology for manufacture, combining these with craft skills to create individual work across homeware, furniture, interiors and installations. It was founded in 2002 by Claire Warnier and Dries Verbruggen, after they graduated from the Design Academy Eindhoven. The Antwerp-based duo developed a strong multidisciplinary background in design, technology and art, and collaborate with a wide network of fellow artists and specialists.

UUFIE

UUfie is an innovative architecture and design studio based in Toronto and working internationally. They provide architectural design services, from concept to construction, as well as interior, urban, landscape and exhibition design services. Current projects range in scale and type from private houses to major commercial and cultural projects in Europe, Asia and North America. Additionally, they experiment with new material technologies to create their one-off projects, such as furniture pieces.

DIRK VANDER KOOIJ

Dirk Vander Kooij is a designer and a craftsman, although most of the objects he produces are not made by hand. He is instead a new kind of craftsman, embracing technology and machines, but not in the same way that industrial producers embrace their manufacturing lines. He studied at the Design Academy in Eindhoven from 2005 to 2010, where his graduation assignment was inspired by an old 3D-printer. Kooij was one of the early pioneers in successfully printing large-scale objects as single volumes.

IRIS VAN HERPEN

Dutch fashion designer Iris Van Herpen's fantastical style encompasses haute couture and cutting-edge technology. She studied Fashion Design at ArtEZ Institute of the Arts, Arnhem, and interned at Alexander McQueen, London, and Claudy Jongstra, Amsterdam. In 2007 she established her own label, and since 2011 has been a guest member of the prestigious Chambre syndicale de la haute couture, Paris. Van Herpen regularly collaborates with other pioneering designers across architecture, fashion, technology and the fine arts.

ERIC VAN STRAATEN

After working for years in wax and resin, sculptural artist Eric van Straaten now works extensively on digital sculptures for advanced 3D-printing. He sees 3D-printing techniques as a means of achieving limitless freedom in creating anything he can imagine. After six years learning how to prepare 3D models for additive manufacturing, with a focus on the latest multi-colour print capabilities, Van Straaten offers his expertise as a consultant to other artists and individuals, and is listed as a design expert on consumer-facing 3D-printing platforms such as i.materialise.

MICHAELLA JANSE VAN VUUREN

With a PhD in Electrical Engineering, South African designer and artist Michaella Janse van Vuuren has been involved in 3D-printing since completing her Postdoctorate in Custom Implant Design in 2006. She has combined her engineering expertise with art and design, exploring creative ideas and processes through many different disciplines, designing lighting, jewelry, accessories and acclaimed artworks. Her 3D-printed designs are exhibited internationally, and are held in the permanent collection of the Science Museum, London.

JEROEN VERHOEVEN

After graduating from Eindhoven Design Academy in 2004, furniture designer Jeroen Verhoeven founded visionary design house Demakersvan with his twin brother Joep Verhoeven and Judith de Graauw. His work has been exhibited internationally, and is in several public and private collections, including the Museum of Modern Art, New York, Victoria & Albert Museum, London, Centre Pompidou, Paris, Art Gallery of Western Australia, Perth, and Die Neue Sammlung, Munich.

MARCEL WANDERS

Dubbed by *The New York Times* as the 'Lady Gaga of Design', Amsterdam-based Marcel Wanders is a prolific product and interior designer and art director, with over 1,700 projects to his name. Regarded by many as an anomaly in the design world, his work excites, provokes and polarizes, but never fails to surprise with its ingenuity and daring. Wanders's chief concern is bringing a human touch back to design, ushering in what he calls design's 'new age', in which designer, craftsman and client are reunited.

JO HAYES WARD

London-based designer Jo Hayes Ward launched her first jewelry collections after graduating with an MA in Goldsmithing, Silversmithing, Metalwork and Jewellery from the Royal College of Art, London. The brand has continued to grow, and her award-winning work is now available internationally at galleries and boutiques. Her work has been exhibited and collected worldwide, and is in the permanent collections of the Crafts Council UK, the Worshipful Company of Goldsmiths and the Alice & Louis Koch Collection, in Switzerland.

WERTELOBERFELL

WertelOberfell was founded in 2007 by Jan Wertel and Gernot Oberfell. Both studied Industrial Design at the Stuttgart State Academy of Art and Design, a school based on the principles of the Ulmer Schule and the Bauhaus, before working for several years for Ross Lovegrove, London. They combine software experiments with the logic and beauty of organic forms and the reality of product design: the right use of materials, production processes and ergonomics. Their work is in the permanent collections of the Metropolitan Museum of Art, New York, and the Victoria & Albert Museum, London.

ZHANG ZHOUJIE

Designer Zhang Zhoujie studied at the China Academy of Art and received an MA in Industrial Design from Central Saint Matins, London. His key working approach is based on 'spontaneity', and pays respect to the logic of mathematics and the laws of the digital environment. He believes that his role as a designer is to be 'actionless', to interfere as little as possible with the natural development of a form. His work blends Chinese traditional art perspectives, Western design methodology, digital engineering and handmade craftsmanship.

ARIEL ZUCKERMAN

Graduating with a BA in Industrial Design from Shenkar College of Engineering, Design and Art, Israel, Ariel Zuckerman is an award-winning product designer. He has designed for many global consumer brands, and his designs have been displayed in exhibitions, museums and galleries, and published around the world. In 2010 Zuckerman formed his own studio, which conceives ranges of consumer products, furniture and lighting. In 2013 he was a finalist at the Israeli Design Awards and won an Excellence Scholarship.

GLOSSARY

3D-PRINTING

Also referred to as additive manufacturing, a collective term for a range of processes used for fabricating objects efficiently and precisely by laying down layers of material, using data taken from a CAD model.

3D-SCANNING

The process of capturing the shape and volume of an object, using a laser to read the surface textures. The data is collated in the form of a three-dimensional CAD model, which can then be manipulated.

BIOMIMETICS

The process of analysing and mimicking the structures of biological organisms – using computer algorithms to realistically simulate natural growth patterns – to find sound solutions to design problems.

CAD (COMPUTER-AIDED DESIGN)

The use of software programs and computer systems to support in the accurate and detailed drawing, modelling, alteration and honing of designs for three-dimensional objects.

CAM (COMPUTER-AIDED MANUFACTURE)

The fabrication of objects using machine tools controlled by computer software and automated systems. Used in conjunction with CAD.

COMPUTATIONAL DESIGN

The process for developing graphic or object designs by applying computer software to calculate and solve problems, creating structurally rigorous or aesthetically perfect solutions.

CNC (COMPUTER NUMERICAL CONTROL)

Term used to define a machine process, controlled by software, for precision manufacturing.

CNC-MILLING

A method of precisely carving a shape from a block of material (such as wood, metal or foam), using fine rotating tools controlled by computer software, which carve on three or five axes to create three-dimensional volumes.

CNC ROUTING

Also called digital routing, a method of precisely cutting material sheets (such as wood, plastic or metal), using fine saws controlled by computer software, which cut on three or five axes to create detailed cutting profiles.

DIGITAL WEAVING

A computer-assisted method of efficiently creating complex textiles, using software to translate a digital design into a weave structure – each pixel is allocated to a defined thread on the digital loom, as chosen by the artisan.

DIGITAL KNITTING

A computer-assisted method of creating knitted textiles, using software to translate a digital design by allocating threads to represent the pixels, and controlling the needles of the knitting machine.

DIGITIZING

The process of turning an object into a virtual model, through gathering and processing data that describes its form and physical details.

DIRECT METAL SINTERING

A method through which fine metal powder is fused into a solid object, using a laser beam to melt a layer of powder at a time and build up the form, without the need of a mould to cast the metal.

DISTRIBUTED MANUFACTURING

Also called distributed production or local manufacturing, a strategic, coordinated approach to production in which goods are made at the closest workshop to where the order is to be delivered, often on-demand.

FREEFORM MANUFACTURING

Describing the process of creating an object using rapid-prototyping technologies, therefore without imposing the restrictions of moulds or tooling.

FUSED DEPOSITION MODELLING

A method of additive manufacturing where an object is built up from layers of plastic material – from a filament unwound from a coil, melted and extruded through a nozzle. The term is trademarked by Stratasys.

LASER-CUTTING

A method widely used for efficiently cutting sheets of material into complex shapes – including metals, plastics, wood, cardboard and textiles – using a focused, computer-controlled laser beam that results in a clean, precise edge.

LASER-ETCHING

Also called laser engraving, this is the process of tracing fine, permanent lines in the surface of a material – usually metal or wood – using precisely focused, computer-controlled lasers that vaporize or fracture the surface.

LATHING

A process used in wood and metalworking to create symmetrical, volumetric forms. As the object is rotated around a central axis, the surface is carved away by a grope, guided by a 2D profile template.

LOST-WAX METHOD

A method of making moulds for casting metal objects. A wax model of the object is encased in a plaster mould, which is then placed into a furnace. The wax is incinerated and the resulting mould cleaned out.

MASS CUSTOMIZATION

The creation of individual products, with details personalized for the end user, using digital manufacturing technologies to make them available at the affordability and scale of mass produced products.

PHOTOCHEMICAL ETCHING

A process of carving away highly complex details in a metal sheet, using a combination of protective layers and corrosive chemicals. Originally used in electronic circuit board manufacture.

RAPID-PROTOTYPING

A collective term for the process of fabricating finished objects or prototypes, by translating 3D CAD models into physical form using 3D-printing or additive layer manufacturing technologies. Rapid-prototyping is much quicker, more efficient and exact than making prototypes through traditional hand-methods.

RENDERING

The process of creating a complete image of an object in a computer program, including the patterns, textures, details and effects of lighting on the surface of the three-dimensional model.

REVERSE ENGINEERING

The process of inspecting or dissecting a physical object, to analyse how it is made, in order to create a new or improved digital model for manufacturing similar objects.

ROTATIONAL MOULDING

A measure of moulten material, such as glass or plastic, is placed into a heated, hollow mould. The mould is rotated around two axes so the material disperses across the internal surfaces to create a final, hollow object.

SELECTIVE LASER-SINTERING

Also known as laser-sintering. A 3D-printing technique where an object is built up from 0.1 mm layers of material powder – either plastic or metal – and fused into a solid using a laser beam. The surrounding unfused powder acts as a support that is later brushed away.

STEREOLITHOGRAPHY

A method of 3D-printing where an object is built up in layers of photopolymer resin – a flatbed sinks slowly into a tank of liquid resin, the surface of which is cured with a UV laser to build up the solid layers of the object.

PHOTO CREDITS

For Grandad, in whose steps I follow.
Love and thank you to my family, and to Beau the whippet
for his ever-enthusiastic company.

First published in the United Kingdom in 2015 by Thames & Hudson Ltd,
181A High Holborn, London WC1V 7QX

Digital Handmade: Craftsmanship in the New Industrial Revolution
© 2015 Lucy Johnston

British Library Cataloguing-in-Publication Data
A catalogue record for this book is available from the British Library

ISBN 978-0-500-51785-7

Printed and bound in China by HK Graphics and Printing Ltd

To find out about all our publications, please visit **www.thamesandhudson.com**.
There you can subscribe to our e-newsletter, browse or download our current catalogue,
and buy any titles that are in print.